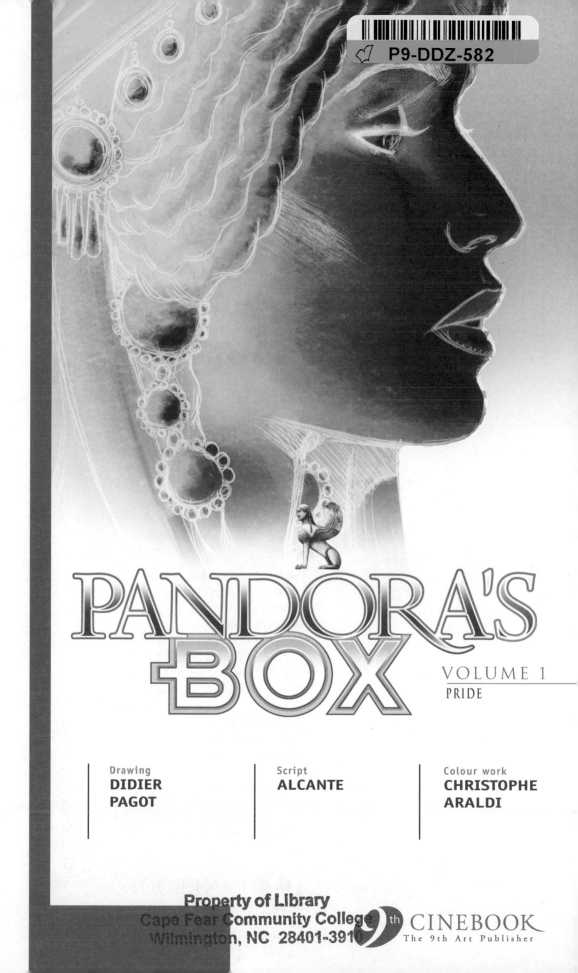

PANDORA'S BOX

VOLUME 1
PRIDE

Drawing
**DIDIER
PAGOT**

Script
ALCANTE

Colour work
**CHRISTOPHE
ARALDI**

CINEBOOK
The 9th Art Publisher

Narcissus

A young man gifted with great beauty, he fell in love
with his own reflection in the water of a spring.
When he tried to kiss it, he fell into the water and drowned.
On the spot where he died grew the flower that bears his name.

Pandora's Box

Of Pride, like Narcissus, you will pay the heavy price.
Of Sloth, like Paris, you will succumb to the slow venom.
Of Gluttony, like Theseus, you will know the foul torment.
Of Lust, like Orpheus, you will bite the bitter fruit.
Of Greed, like Midas, you will learn the hard law.
Of Envy, like Prometheus, you will suffer the eternal punishment.
Of Wrath, like Pandora, you will be the fatal instrument.

Finally, at the very end,
Your soul seven times destroyed,
Only hope will remain,
To live and rise again.

Thus spoke the Oracle
When the box was opened
And its savage spice
Into the world had spread.

Original title: Pandora Box 1 – L'orgueil
Original edition: © Dupuis, 2005 by Pagot & Alcante
www.dupuis.com
All rights reserved
English translation: © 2008 Cinebook Ltd
Translator: Jerome Saincantin
Lettering and text layout: Imadjinn
Printed in Spain by Just Colour Graphic
This edition first published in Great Britain in 2009 by
CINEBOOK Ltd
56 Beech Avenue
Canterbury, Kent
CT4 7TA
www.cinebook.com
A CIP catalogue record for this book
is available from the British Library
ISBN 978-1-905460-81-6

9th CINEBOOK
The 9th Art Publisher

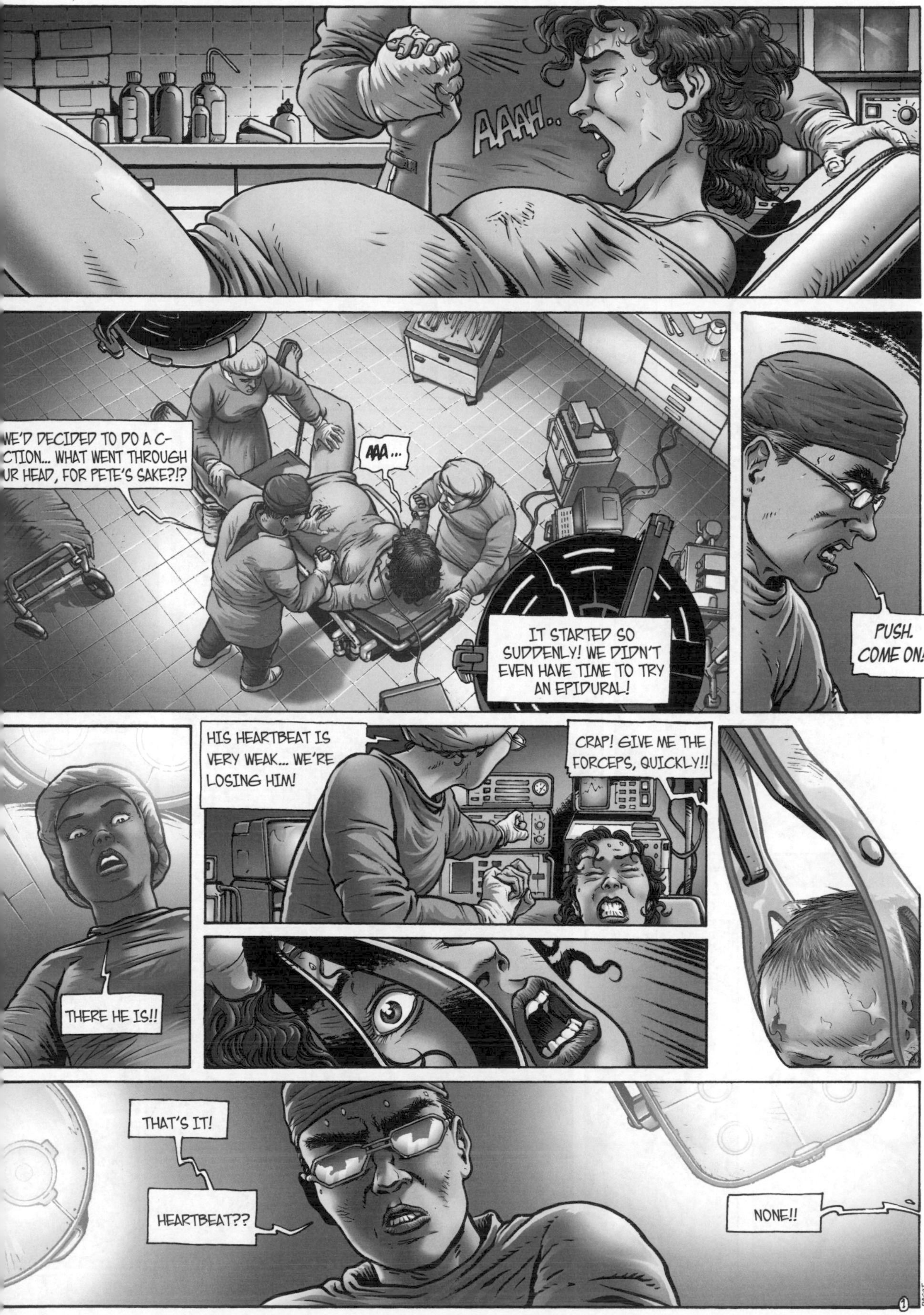
AAAH..
WE'D DECIDED TO DO A C-CTION... WHAT WENT THROUGH UR HEAD, FOR PETE'S SAKE?!?
AAA...
IT STARTED SO SUDDENLY! WE DIDN'T EVEN HAVE TIME TO TRY AN EPIDURAL!
PUSH. COME ON!!
THERE HE IS!!
HIS HEARTBEAT IS VERY WEAK... WE'RE LOSING HIM!
CRAP! GIVE ME THE FORCEPS, QUICKLY!!
THAT'S IT!
HEARTBEAT??
NONE!!

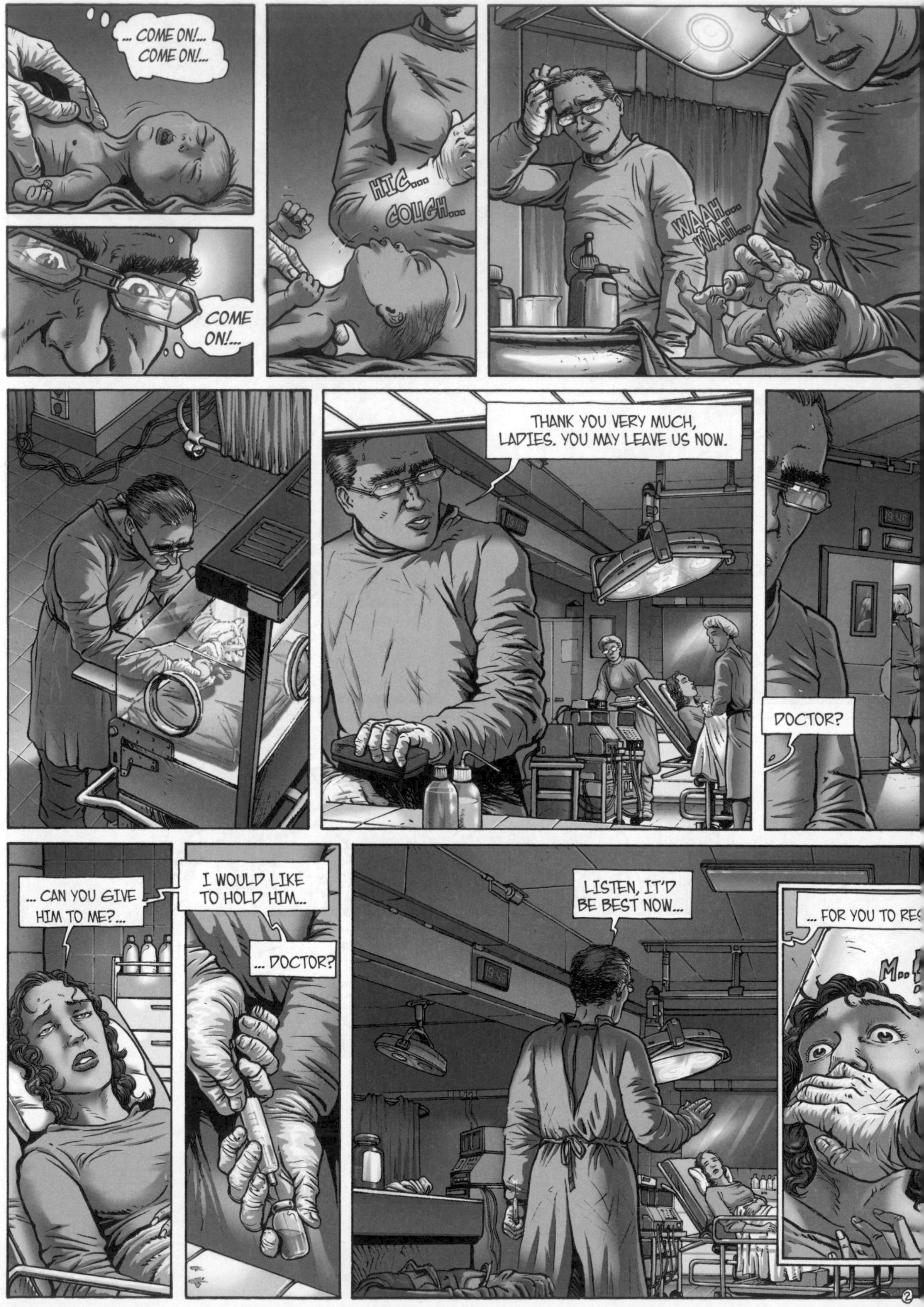
... COME ON!... COME ON!...
COME ON!...
HIC... COUGH...
WAAH... WAAH...
THANK YOU VERY MUCH, LADIES. YOU MAY LEAVE US NOW.
DOCTOR?
... CAN YOU GIVE HIM TO ME?...
I WOULD LIKE TO HOLD HIM...
... DOCTOR?
LISTEN, IT'D BE BEST NOW...
... FOR YOU TO RE

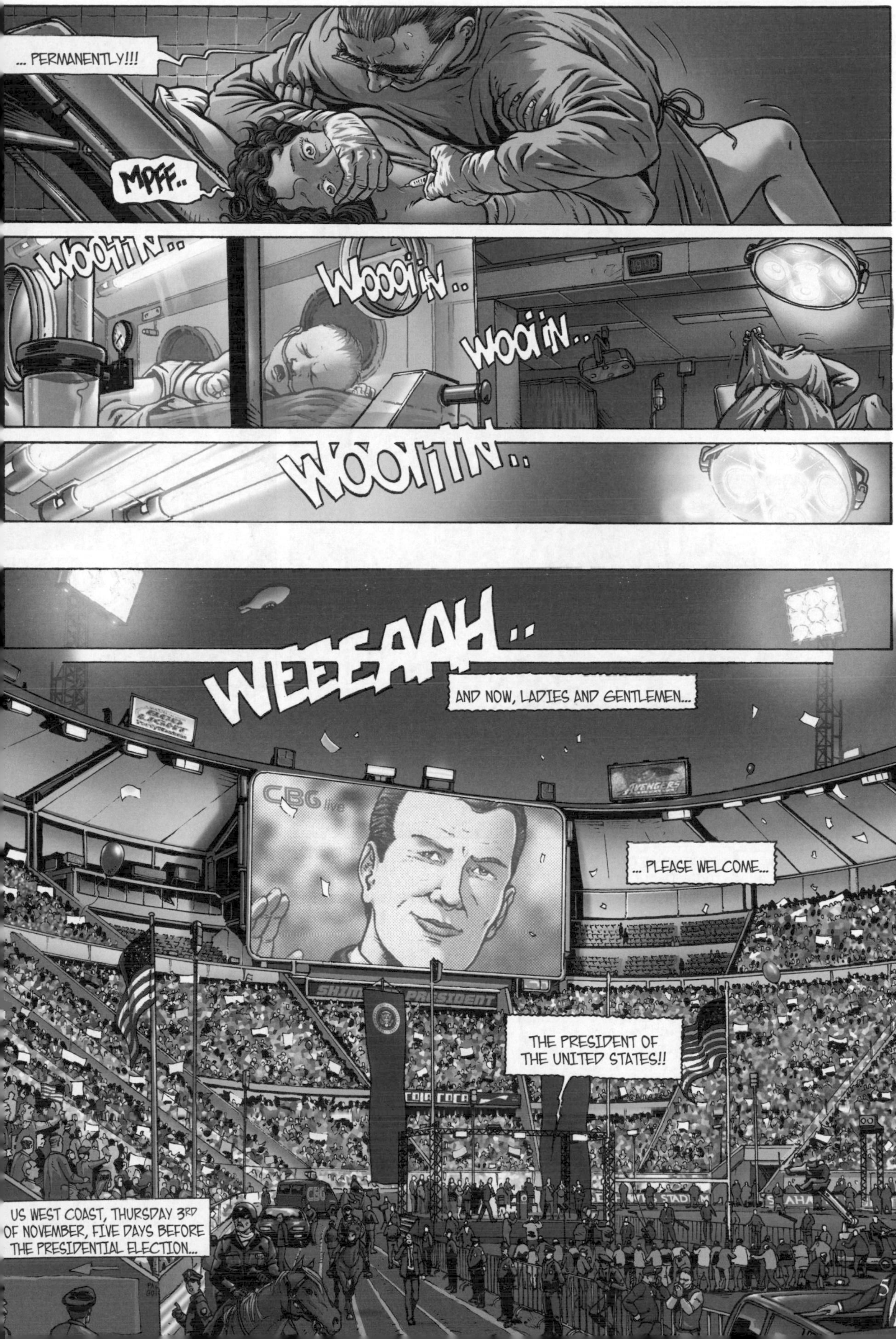
... PERMANENTLY!!!
MPFF..
WOOI'IN..
WOOOI'IN..
WOOI'IN..
WOOI'IIN..
WEEEAAH..
AND NOW, LADIES AND GENTLEMEN...
... PLEASE WELCOME...
THE PRESIDENT OF THE UNITED STATES!!
US WEST COAST, THURSDAY 3RD OF NOVEMBER, FIVE DAYS BEFORE THE PRESIDENTIAL ELECTION...

YOU KNOW HIM, OF COURSE. NARCISSUS SHIMMER, 52, MARRIED, ONE SON, CURRENT PRESIDENT OF THE UNITED STATES AND HIS PARTY'S CANDIDATE FOR RE-ELECTION.

... CLAIRE DALE. HIS CAMPAIGN MANAGER. SHE'S DONE A REMARKABLE JOB, YOU HAVE TO ADMIT.

THE RESULT: SHIMMER JUST OVERTOOK ME IN THE POLLS! A MERE FIVE DAYS BEFORE THE ELECTION. YOU'LL UNDERSTAND THAT I FIND THIS A SERIOUS INCONVENIENCE!!

... IF SHIMMER WINS, HE'LL USE HIS SECOND MANDATE TO FINISH THE GREAT WORKS HE STARTED. HIS PARTY WILL BE MORE POPULAR THAN EVER. AND IN FOUR YEARS, THE VICE PRESIDENT WILL SUCCEED HIM. OUR PARTY CANNOT AFFORD IT!...

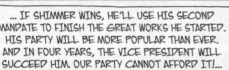

... WHICH IS WHY WE HAVE CALLED UPON YOU...

... MR GRUBB.

IN FOUR DAYS, THE DAY BEFORE THE ELECTION, THERE WILL BE A LIVE DEBATE BETWEEN THE TWO CANDIDATES. IT WILL BE THE LAST CHANCE TO TURN THE SITUATION AROUND. FIND SOMETHING AND WE'LL ANNOUNCE IT LIVE ON TV!

WE'RE SO CLOSE TO EACH OTHER IN THE POLLS THAT A LAST-MINUTE SCANDAL COULDN'T FAIL TO GIVE ME A VICTORY.

WHY DID YOU WAIT SO LONG BEFORE CALLING UPON MY SERVICES?

I TOLD YOU. SHIMMER JUST GOT AHEAD IN THE POLLS IN THE LAST FEW DAYS.

WHAT DO YOU HAVE ON HIM AT THE MOMENT?

ALMOST NOTHING. WE ONLY FOUND INCONSEQUENTIAL THINGS, NOTHING MORE THAN WHAT THEY ALREADY KNOW ABOUT ME. THERE'S GOT TO BE SOMETHING MORE! I WANT YOU TO SEARCH THROUGH HIS SHIT UNTIL YOU FIND IT. YOU'RE SUPPOSED TO BE THE BEST AT THAT KIND OF WORK.

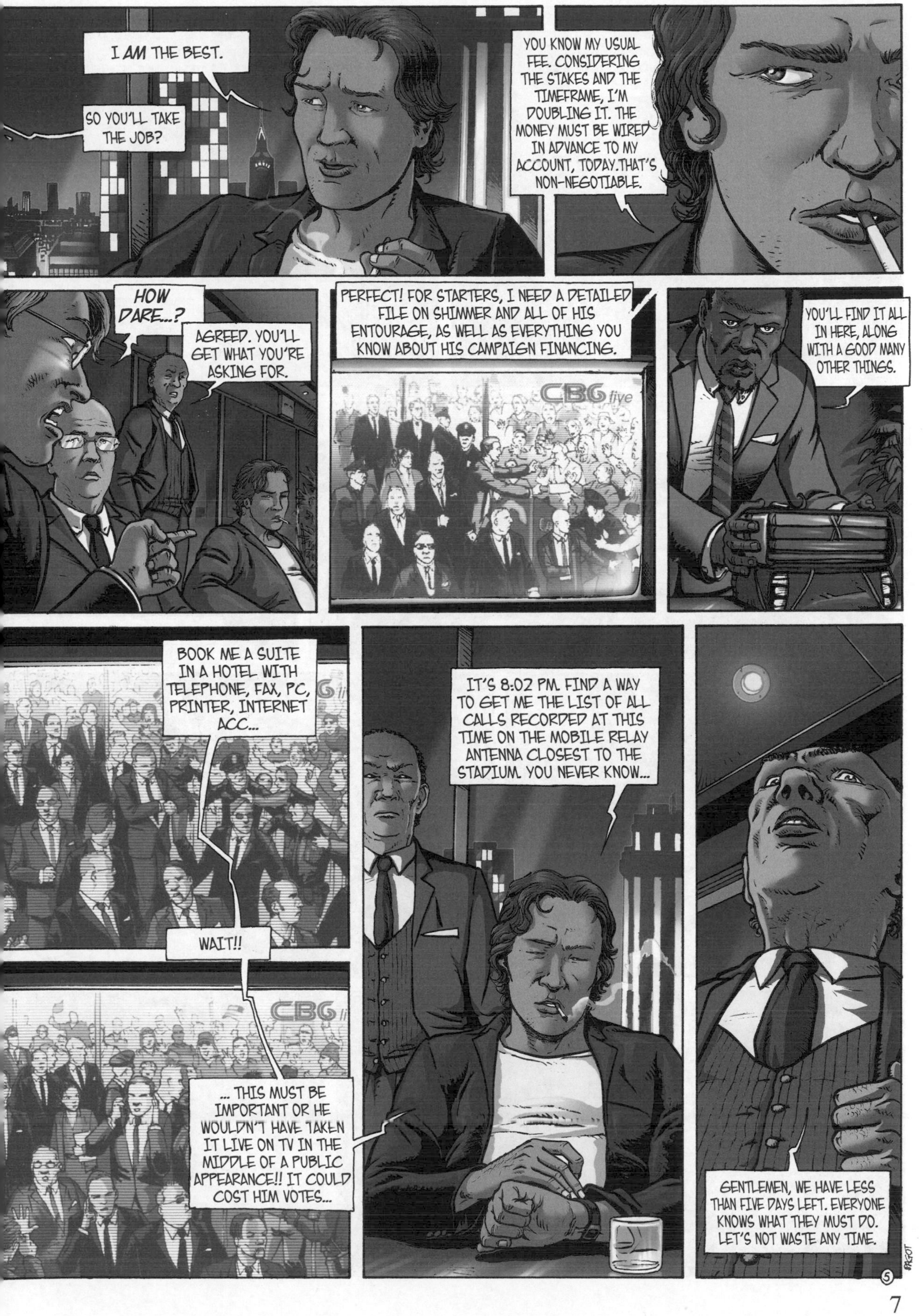
I AM THE BEST.
SO YOU'LL TAKE THE JOB?
YOU KNOW MY USUAL FEE. CONSIDERING THE STAKES AND THE TIMEFRAME, I'M DOUBLING IT. THE MONEY MUST BE WIRED IN ADVANCE TO MY ACCOUNT, TODAY.THAT'S NON-NEGOTIABLE.
HOW DARE...?
AGREED. YOU'LL GET WHAT YOU'RE ASKING FOR.
PERFECT! FOR STARTERS, I NEED A DETAILED FILE ON SHIMMER AND ALL OF HIS ENTOURAGE, AS WELL AS EVERYTHING YOU KNOW ABOUT HIS CAMPAIGN FINANCING.
CBG live
YOU'LL FIND IT ALL IN HERE, ALONG WITH A GOOD MANY OTHER THINGS.
BOOK ME A SUITE IN A HOTEL WITH TELEPHONE, FAX, PC, PRINTER, INTERNET ACC...
WAIT!!
... THIS MUST BE IMPORTANT OR HE WOULDN'T HAVE TAKEN IT LIVE ON TV IN THE MIDDLE OF A PUBLIC APPEARANCE!! IT COULD COST HIM VOTES...
IT'S 8:02 PM. FIND A WAY TO GET ME THE LIST OF ALL CALLS RECORDED AT THIS TIME ON THE MOBILE RELAY ANTENNA CLOSEST TO THE STADIUM. YOU NEVER KNOW...
GENTLEMEN, WE HAVE LESS THAN FIVE DAYS LEFT. EVERYONE KNOWS WHAT THEY MUST DO. LET'S NOT WASTE ANY TIME.
5

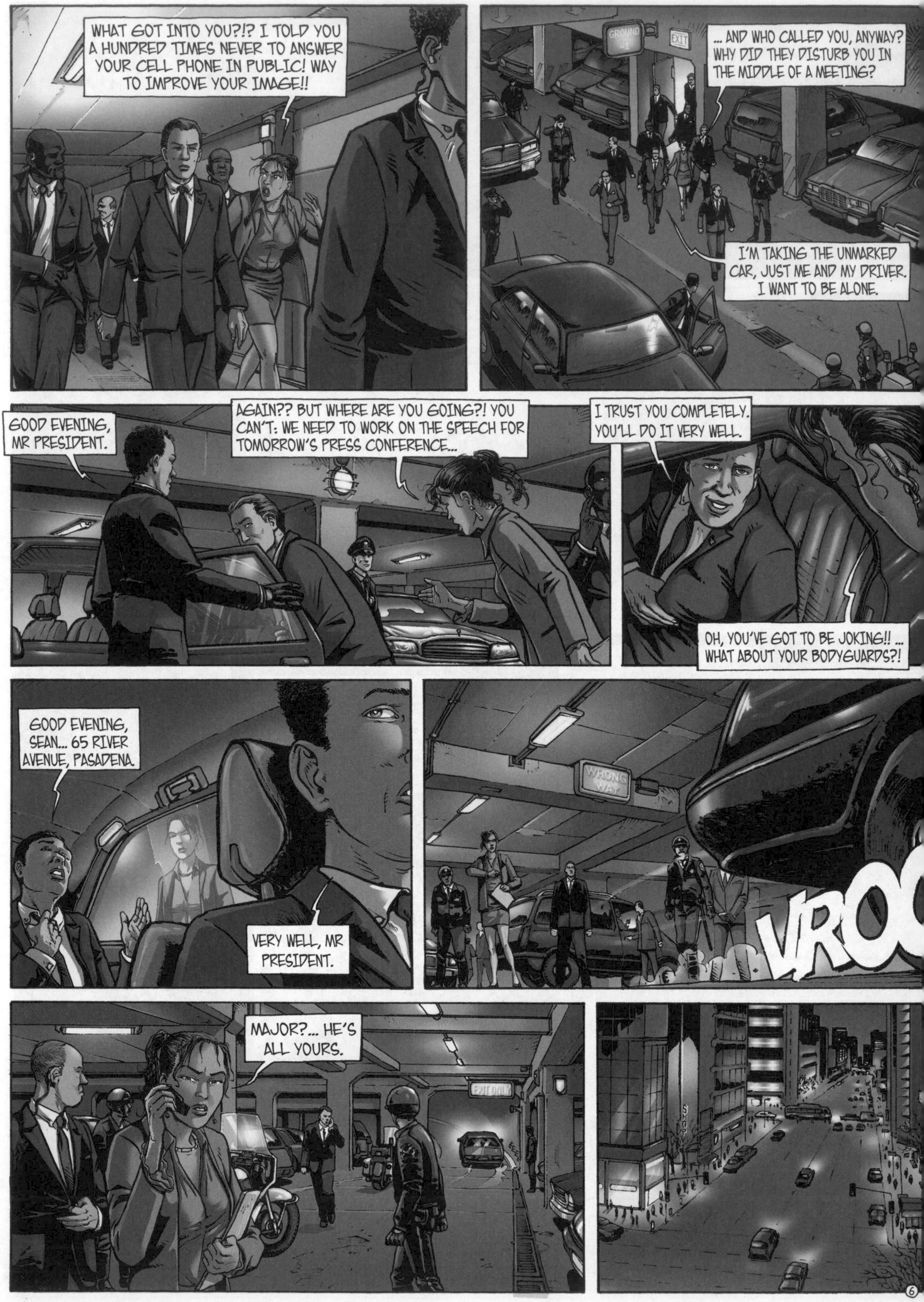
WHAT GOT INTO YOU?!? I TOLD YOU A HUNDRED TIMES NEVER TO ANSWER YOUR CELL PHONE IN PUBLIC! WAY TO IMPROVE YOUR IMAGE!!
GROUND -1
EXIT
... AND WHO CALLED YOU, ANYWAY? WHY DID THEY DISTURB YOU IN THE MIDDLE OF A MEETING?
I'M TAKING THE UNMARKED CAR, JUST ME AND MY DRIVER. I WANT TO BE ALONE.
GOOD EVENING, MR PRESIDENT.
AGAIN?? BUT WHERE ARE YOU GOING?! YOU CAN'T: WE NEED TO WORK ON THE SPEECH FOR TOMORROW'S PRESS CONFERENCE...
I TRUST YOU COMPLETELY. YOU'LL DO IT VERY WELL.
OH, YOU'VE GOT TO BE JOKING!! ... WHAT ABOUT YOUR BODYGUARDS?!
GOOD EVENING, SEAN... 65 RIVER AVENUE, PASADENA.
VERY WELL, MR PRESIDENT.
WRONG WAY
VROO
MAJOR?... HE'S ALL YOURS.
EXIT ONLY
6

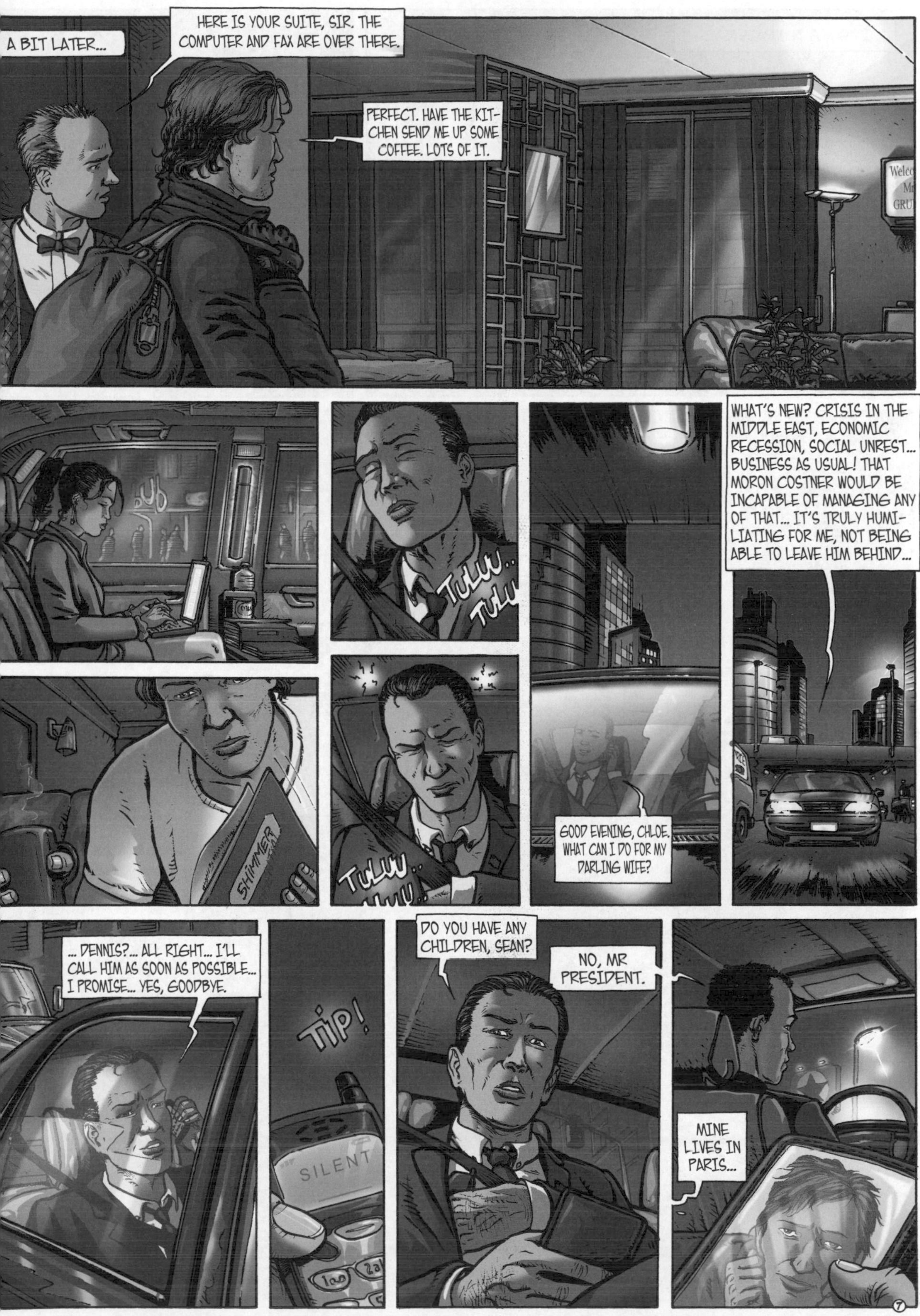
A BIT LATER...
HERE IS YOUR SUITE, SIR. THE COMPUTER AND FAX ARE OVER THERE.
PERFECT. HAVE THE KITCHEN SEND ME UP SOME COFFEE. LOTS OF IT.
TULUU.. TULU
SHIMMER
GOOD EVENING, CHLOE. WHAT CAN I DO FOR MY DARLING WIFE?
WHAT'S NEW? CRISIS IN THE MIDDLE EAST, ECONOMIC RECESSION, SOCIAL UNREST... BUSINESS AS USUAL! THAT MORON COSTNER WOULD BE INCAPABLE OF MANAGING ANY OF THAT... IT'S TRULY HUMILIATING FOR ME, NOT BEING ABLE TO LEAVE HIM BEHIND...
... DENNIS?... ALL RIGHT... I'LL CALL HIM AS SOON AS POSSIBLE... I PROMISE... YES, GOODBYE.
TIP!
SILENT
DO YOU HAVE ANY CHILDREN, SEAN?
NO, MR PRESIDENT.
MINE LIVES IN PARIS...

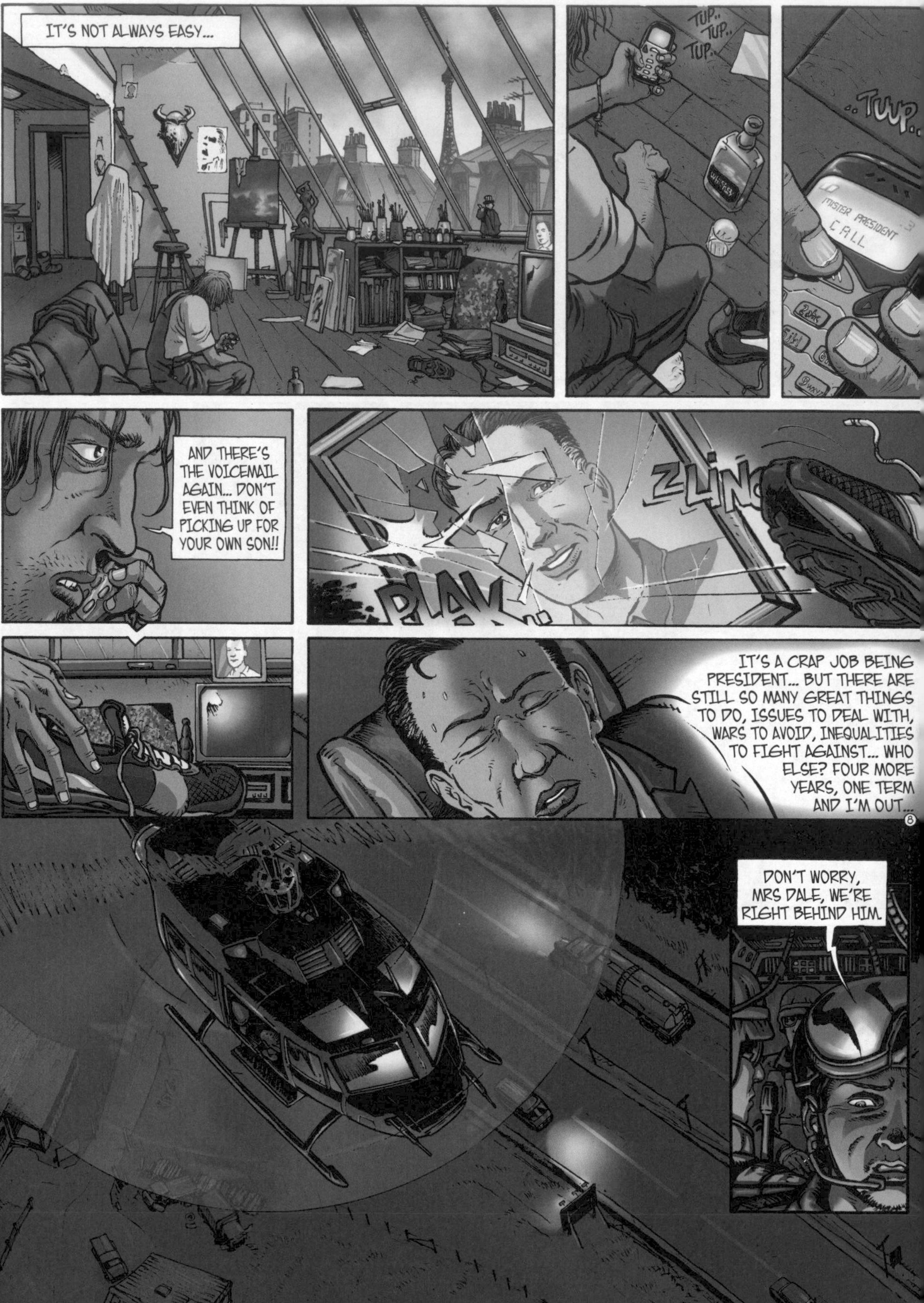
IT'S NOT ALWAYS EASY...
TUP.. TUP.. TUP..
MISTER PRESIDENT
CALL
..TUUP..
AND THERE'S THE VOICEMAIL AGAIN... DON'T EVEN THINK OF PICKING UP FOR YOUR OWN SON!!
ZLING
PLAK
IT'S A CRAP JOB BEING PRESIDENT... BUT THERE ARE STILL SO MANY GREAT THINGS TO DO, ISSUES TO DEAL WITH, WARS TO AVOID, INEQUALITIES TO FIGHT AGAINST... WHO ELSE? FOUR MORE YEARS, ONE TERM AND I'M OUT...
DON'T WORRY, MRS DALE, WE'RE RIGHT BEHIND HIM.

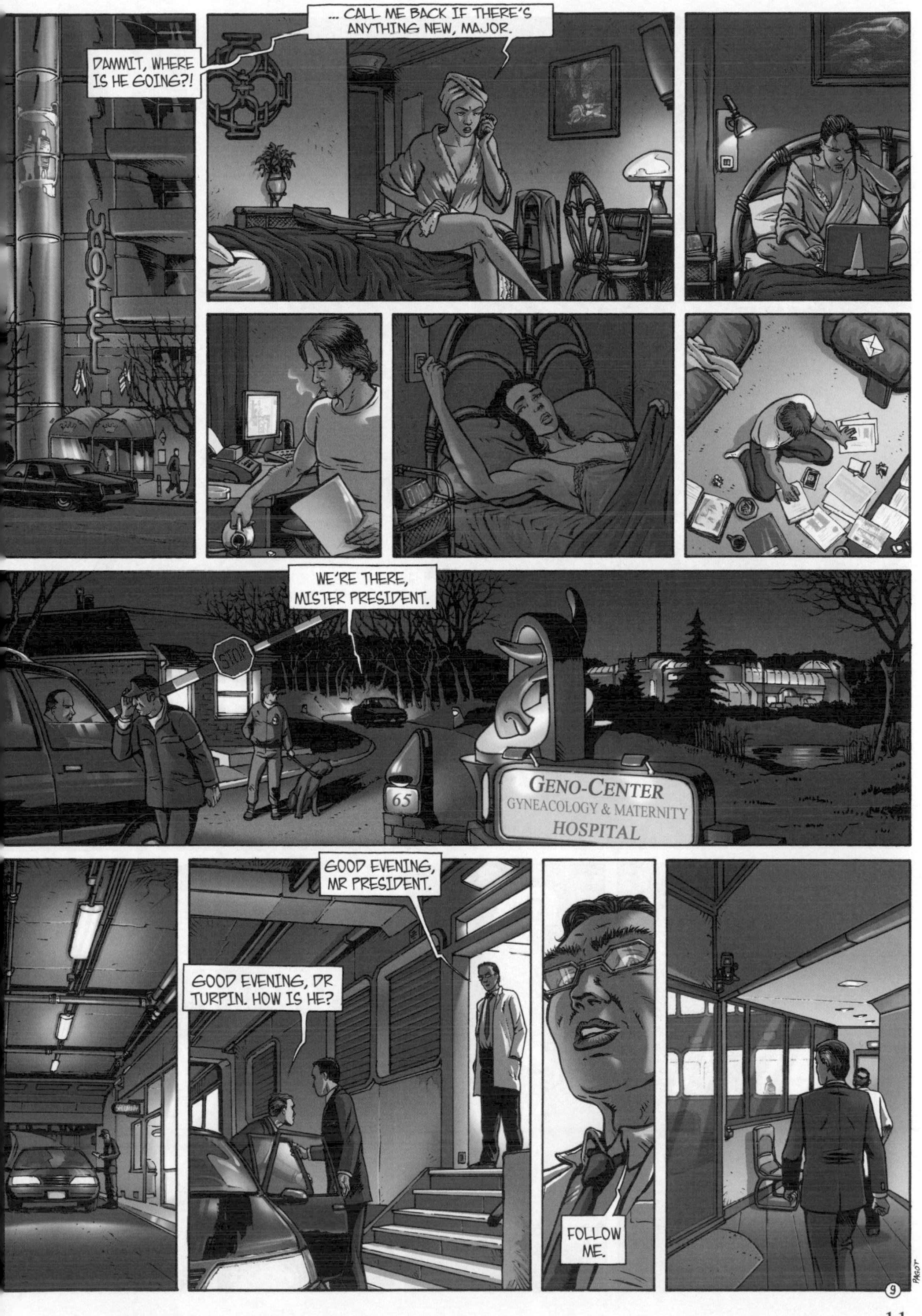
DAMMIT, WHERE IS HE GOING?!
... CALL ME BACK IF THERE'S ANYTHING NEW, MAJOR.
STOP
WE'RE THERE, MISTER PRESIDENT.
65
GENO-CENTER
GYNEACOLOGY & MATERNITY
HOSPITAL
GOOD EVENING, MR PRESIDENT.
GOOD EVENING, DR TURPIN. HOW IS HE?
FOLLOW ME.
PAGOT
9

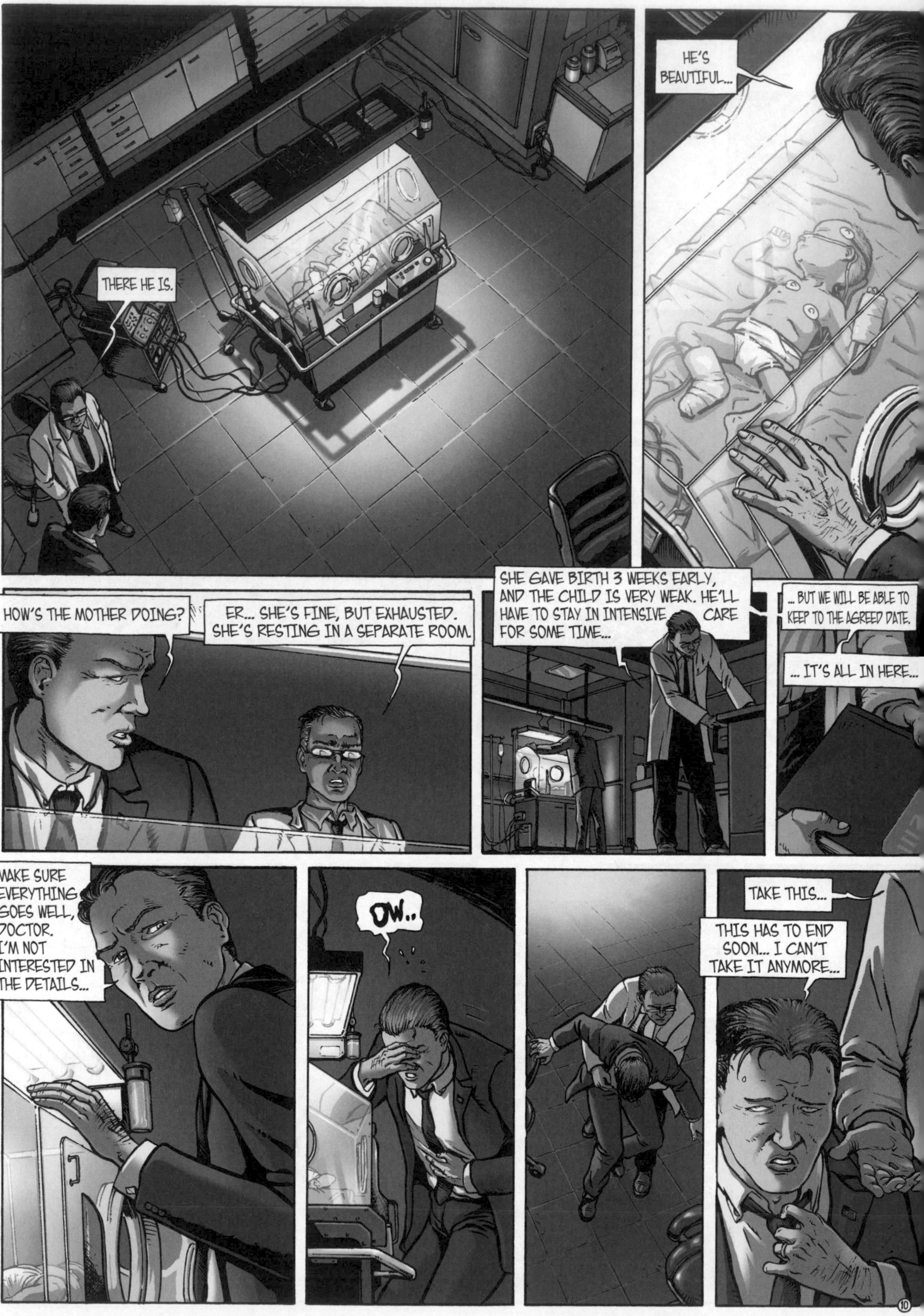
THERE HE IS.
HE'S BEAUTIFUL...
HOW'S THE MOTHER DOING?
ER... SHE'S FINE, BUT EXHAUSTED. SHE'S RESTING IN A SEPARATE ROOM.
SHE GAVE BIRTH 3 WEEKS EARLY, AND THE CHILD IS VERY WEAK. HE'LL HAVE TO STAY IN INTENSIVE CARE FOR SOME TIME...
... BUT WE WILL BE ABLE TO KEEP TO THE AGREED DATE.
... IT'S ALL IN HERE...
MAKE SURE EVERYTHING GOES WELL, DOCTOR. I'M NOT INTERESTED IN THE DETAILS...
OW..
TAKE THIS...
THIS HAS TO END SOON... I CAN'T TAKE IT ANYMORE...
10

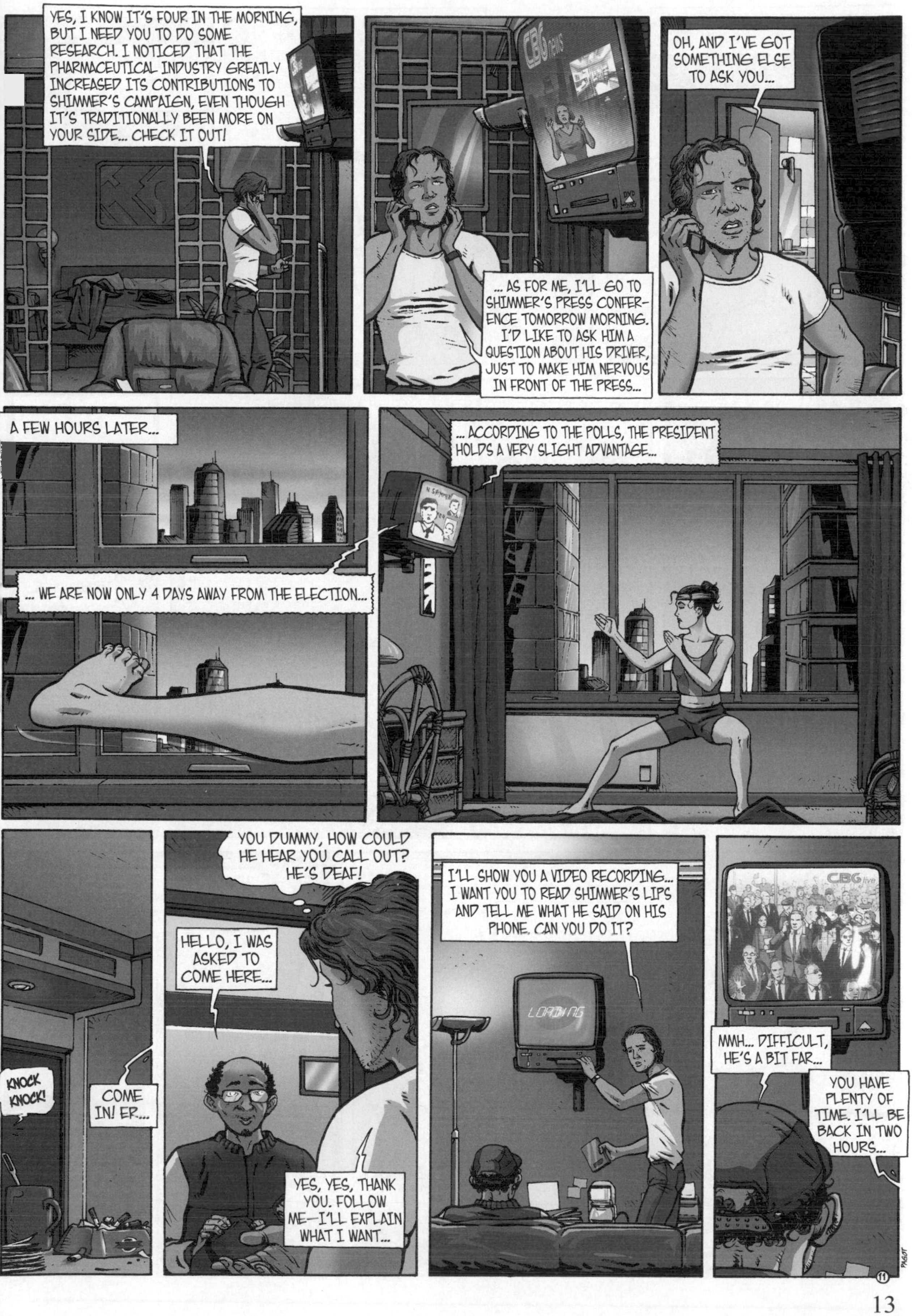
YES, I KNOW IT'S FOUR IN THE MORNING, BUT I NEED YOU TO DO SOME RESEARCH. I NOTICED THAT THE PHARMACEUTICAL INDUSTRY GREATLY INCREASED ITS CONTRIBUTIONS TO SHIMMER'S CAMPAIGN, EVEN THOUGH IT'S TRADITIONALLY BEEN MORE ON YOUR SIDE... CHECK IT OUT!
... AS FOR ME, I'LL GO TO SHIMMER'S PRESS CONFERENCE TOMORROW MORNING. I'D LIKE TO ASK HIM A QUESTION ABOUT HIS DRIVER, JUST TO MAKE HIM NERVOUS IN FRONT OF THE PRESS...
OH, AND I'VE GOT SOMETHING ELSE TO ASK YOU...
A FEW HOURS LATER...
... WE ARE NOW ONLY 4 DAYS AWAY FROM THE ELECTION...
... ACCORDING TO THE POLLS, THE PRESIDENT HOLDS A VERY SLIGHT ADVANTAGE...
KNOCK KNOCK!
COME IN! ER...
YOU DUMMY, HOW COULD HE HEAR YOU CALL OUT? HE'S DEAF!
HELLO, I WAS ASKED TO COME HERE...
YES, YES, THANK YOU. FOLLOW ME—I'LL EXPLAIN WHAT I WANT...
I'LL SHOW YOU A VIDEO RECORDING... I WANT YOU TO READ SHIMMER'S LIPS AND TELL ME WHAT HE SAID ON HIS PHONE. CAN YOU DO IT?
MMH... DIFFICULT, HE'S A BIT FAR...
YOU HAVE PLENTY OF TIME. I'LL BE BACK IN TWO HOURS...

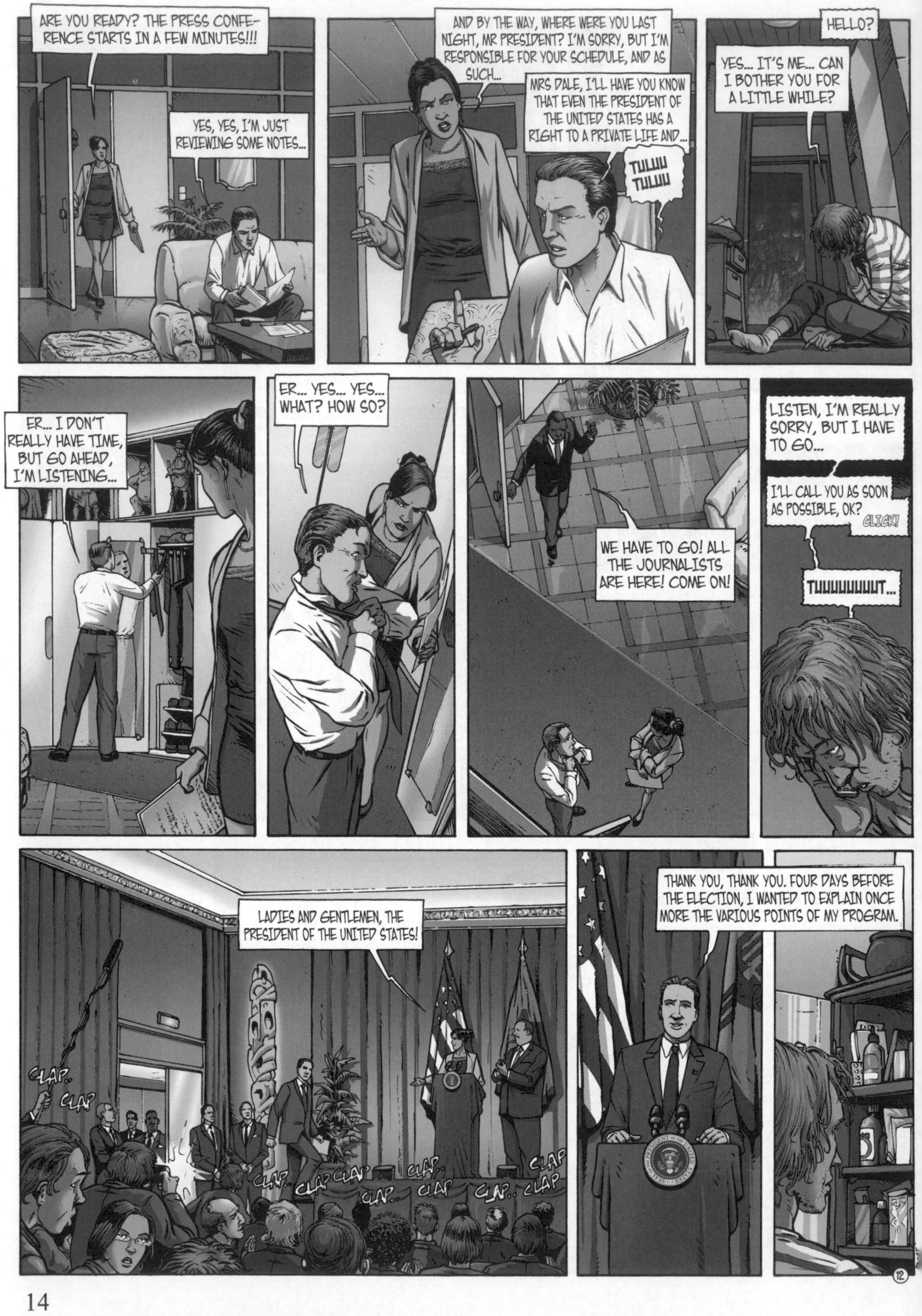
ARE YOU READY? THE PRESS CONFERENCE STARTS IN A FEW MINUTES!!!
YES, YES, I'M JUST REVIEWING SOME NOTES...
AND BY THE WAY, WHERE WERE YOU LAST NIGHT, MR PRESIDENT? I'M SORRY, BUT I'M RESPONSIBLE FOR YOUR SCHEDULE, AND AS SUCH...
MRS DALE, I'LL HAVE YOU KNOW THAT EVEN THE PRESIDENT OF THE UNITED STATES HAS A RIGHT TO A PRIVATE LIFE AND...
TULUU TULUU
HELLO?
YES... IT'S ME... CAN I BOTHER YOU FOR A LITTLE WHILE?
ER... I DON'T REALLY HAVE TIME, BUT GO AHEAD, I'M LISTENING...
ER... YES... YES... WHAT? HOW SO?
WE HAVE TO GO! ALL THE JOURNALISTS ARE HERE! COME ON!
LISTEN, I'M REALLY SORRY, BUT I HAVE TO GO...
I'LL CALL YOU AS SOON AS POSSIBLE, OK?
CLICK!
TUUUUUUUUT...
LADIES AND GENTLEMEN, THE PRESIDENT OF THE UNITED STATES!
CLAP.. CLAP
CLAP.. CLAP CLAP CLAP.. CLAP.. CLAP CLAP.. CLAP CLAP.. CLAP CLAP
THANK YOU, THANK YOU. FOUR DAYS BEFORE THE ELECTION, I WANTED TO EXPLAIN ONCE MORE THE VARIOUS POINTS OF MY PROGRAM.
12

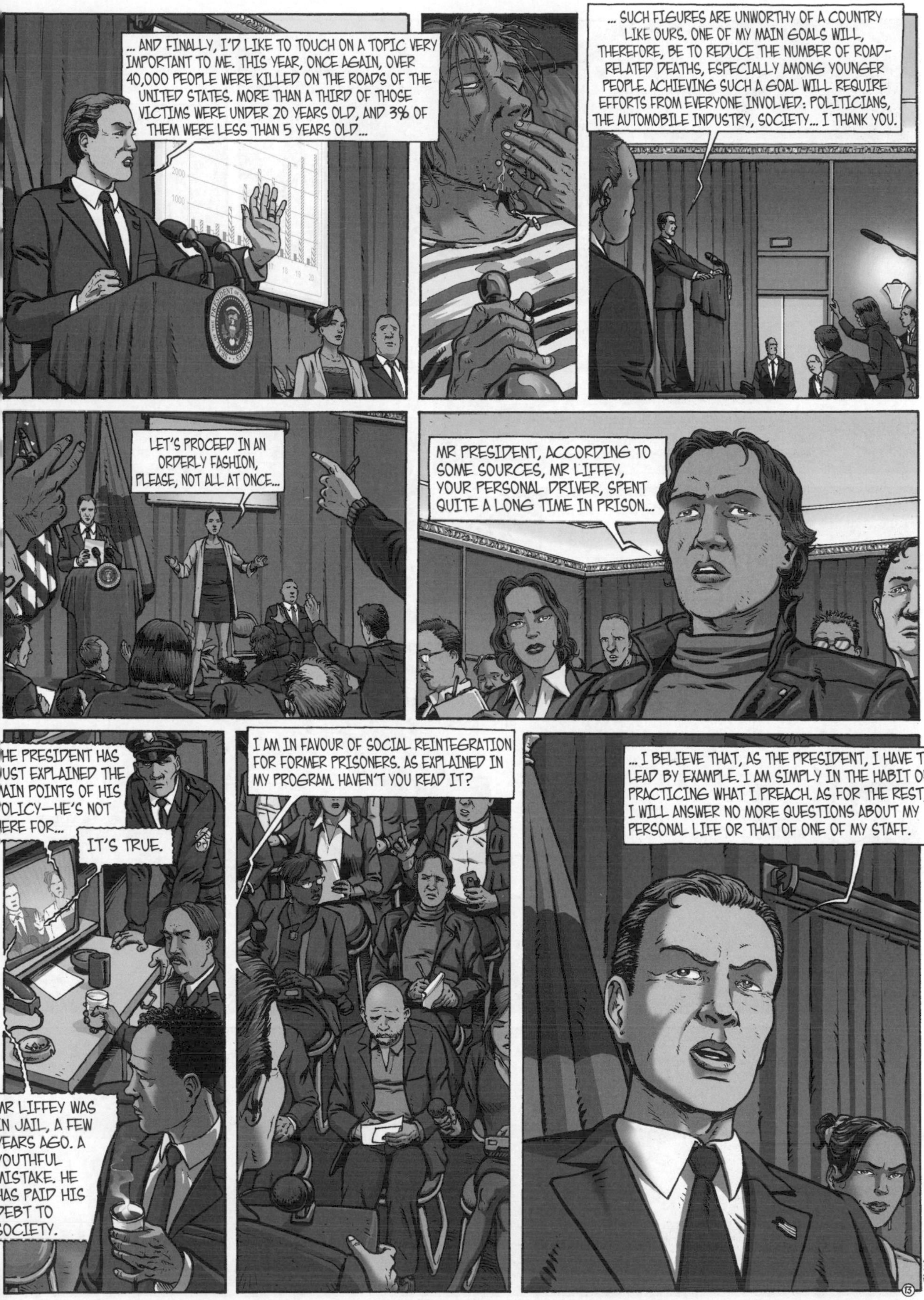
... AND FINALLY, I'D LIKE TO TOUCH ON A TOPIC VERY IMPORTANT TO ME. THIS YEAR, ONCE AGAIN, OVER 40,000 PEOPLE WERE KILLED ON THE ROADS OF THE UNITED STATES. MORE THAN A THIRD OF THOSE VICTIMS WERE UNDER 20 YEARS OLD, AND 3% OF THEM WERE LESS THAN 5 YEARS OLD...
... SUCH FIGURES ARE UNWORTHY OF A COUNTRY LIKE OURS. ONE OF MY MAIN GOALS WILL, THEREFORE, BE TO REDUCE THE NUMBER OF ROAD-RELATED DEATHS, ESPECIALLY AMONG YOUNGER PEOPLE. ACHIEVING SUCH A GOAL WILL REQUIRE EFFORTS FROM EVERYONE INVOLVED: POLITICIANS, THE AUTOMOBILE INDUSTRY, SOCIETY... I THANK YOU.
LET'S PROCEED IN AN ORDERLY FASHION, PLEASE, NOT ALL AT ONCE...
MR PRESIDENT, ACCORDING TO SOME SOURCES, MR LIFFEY, YOUR PERSONAL DRIVER, SPENT QUITE A LONG TIME IN PRISON...
HE PRESIDENT HAS UST EXPLAINED THE AIN POINTS OF HIS OLICY—HE'S NOT ERE FOR...
IT'S TRUE.
MR LIFFEY WAS N JAIL, A FEW EARS AGO. A OUTHFUL MISTAKE. HE HAS PAID HIS DEBT TO OCIETY.
I AM IN FAVOUR OF SOCIAL REINTEGRATION FOR FORMER PRISONERS. AS EXPLAINED IN MY PROGRAM. HAVEN'T YOU READ IT?
... I BELIEVE THAT, AS THE PRESIDENT, I HAVE TO LEAD BY EXAMPLE. I AM SIMPLY IN THE HABIT OF PRACTICING WHAT I PREACH. AS FOR THE REST, I WILL ANSWER NO MORE QUESTIONS ABOUT MY PERSONAL LIFE OR THAT OF ONE OF MY STAFF.

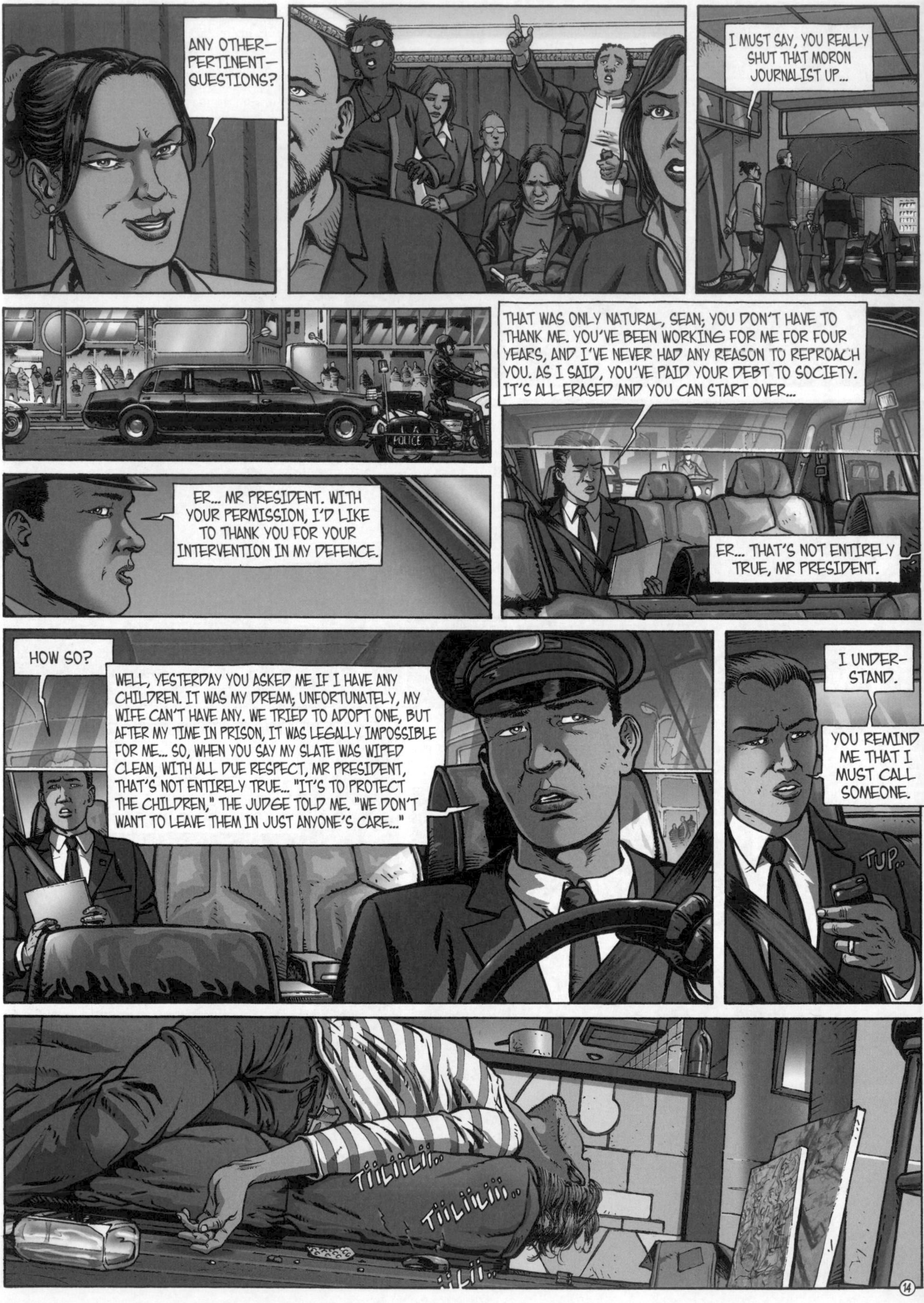
ANY OTHER— PERTINENT— QUESTIONS?
I MUST SAY, YOU REALLY SHUT THAT MORON JOURNALIST UP...
ER... MR PRESIDENT. WITH YOUR PERMISSION, I'D LIKE TO THANK YOU FOR YOUR INTERVENTION IN MY DEFENCE.
THAT WAS ONLY NATURAL, SEAN; YOU DON'T HAVE TO THANK ME. YOU'VE BEEN WORKING FOR ME FOR FOUR YEARS, AND I'VE NEVER HAD ANY REASON TO REPROACH YOU. AS I SAID, YOU'VE PAID YOUR DEBT TO SOCIETY. IT'S ALL ERASED AND YOU CAN START OVER...
ER... THAT'S NOT ENTIRELY TRUE, MR PRESIDENT.
HOW SO?
WELL, YESTERDAY YOU ASKED ME IF I HAVE ANY CHILDREN. IT WAS MY DREAM; UNFORTUNATELY, MY WIFE CAN'T HAVE ANY. WE TRIED TO ADOPT ONE, BUT AFTER MY TIME IN PRISON, IT WAS LEGALLY IMPOSSIBLE FOR ME... SO, WHEN YOU SAY MY SLATE WAS WIPED CLEAN, WITH ALL DUE RESPECT, MR PRESIDENT, THAT'S NOT ENTIRELY TRUE... "IT'S TO PROTECT THE CHILDREN," THE JUDGE TOLD ME. "WE DON'T WANT TO LEAVE THEM IN JUST ANYONE'S CARE..."
I UNDER-STAND.
YOU REMIND ME THAT I MUST CALL SOMEONE.
TUP..
TIILIILII..
TIILIILIII..
iiLii..

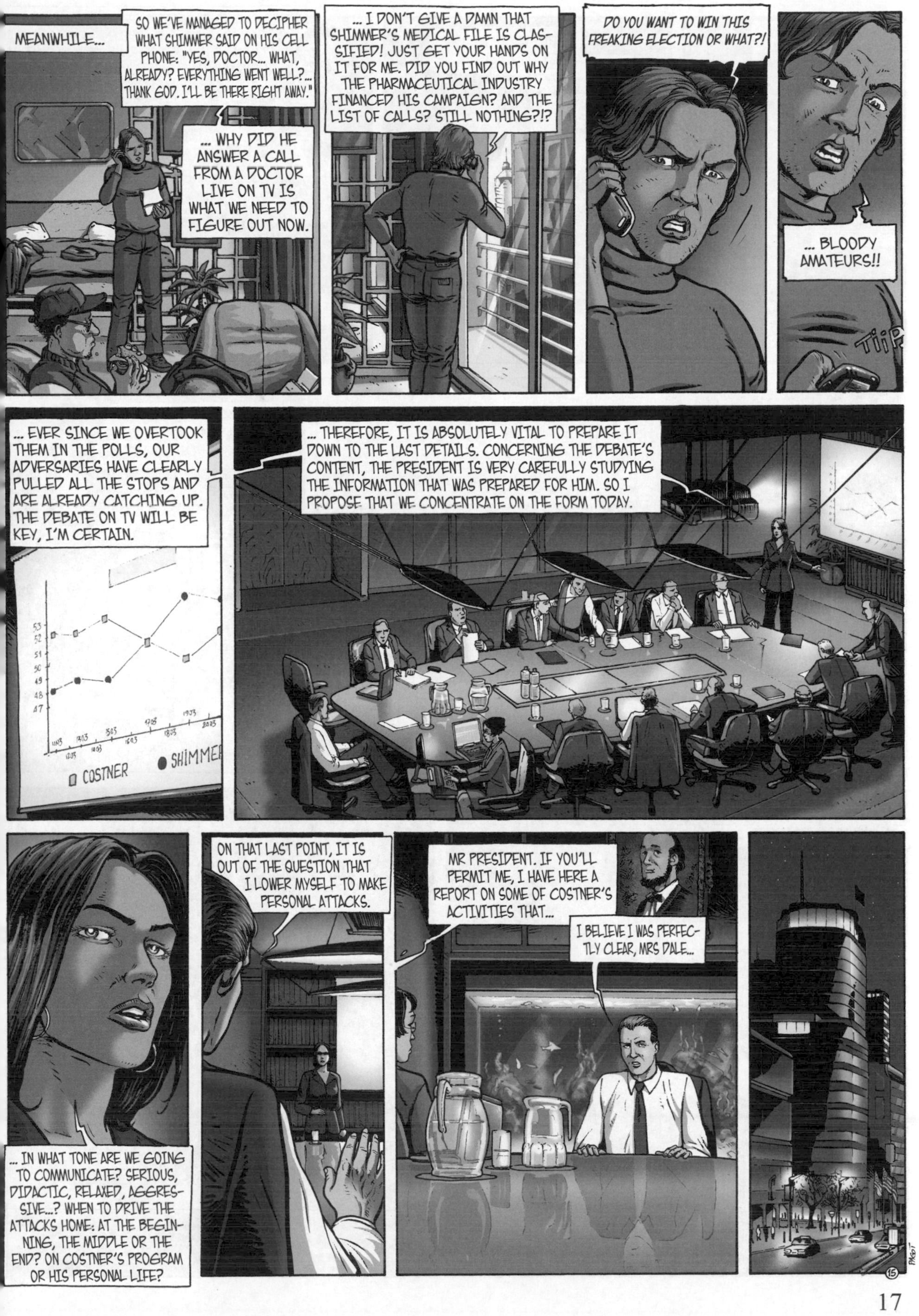
MEANWHILE...
SO WE'VE MANAGED TO DECIPHER WHAT SHIMMER SAID ON HIS CELL PHONE: "YES, DOCTOR... WHAT, ALREADY? EVERYTHING WENT WELL?... THANK GOD. I'LL BE THERE RIGHT AWAY."
... WHY DID HE ANSWER A CALL FROM A DOCTOR LIVE ON TV IS WHAT WE NEED TO FIGURE OUT NOW.
... I DON'T GIVE A DAMN THAT SHIMMER'S MEDICAL FILE IS CLASSIFIED! JUST GET YOUR HANDS ON IT FOR ME. DID YOU FIND OUT WHY THE PHARMACEUTICAL INDUSTRY FINANCED HIS CAMPAIGN? AND THE LIST OF CALLS? STILL NOTHING?!?
DO YOU WANT TO WIN THIS FREAKING ELECTION OR WHAT?!
... BLOODY AMATEURS!!
TiiP
... EVER SINCE WE OVERTOOK THEM IN THE POLLS, OUR ADVERSARIES HAVE CLEARLY PULLED ALL THE STOPS AND ARE ALREADY CATCHING UP. THE DEBATE ON TV WILL BE KEY, I'M CERTAIN.
COSTNER
... THEREFORE, IT IS ABSOLUTELY VITAL TO PREPARE IT DOWN TO THE LAST DETAILS. CONCERNING THE DEBATE'S CONTENT, THE PRESIDENT IS VERY CAREFULLY STUDYING THE INFORMATION THAT WAS PREPARED FOR HIM. SO I PROPOSE THAT WE CONCENTRATE ON THE FORM TODAY.
... IN WHAT TONE ARE WE GOING TO COMMUNICATE? SERIOUS, DIDACTIC, RELAXED, AGGRESSIVE...? WHEN TO DRIVE THE ATTACKS HOME: AT THE BEGINNING, THE MIDDLE OR THE END? ON COSTNER'S PROGRAM OR HIS PERSONAL LIFE?
ON THAT LAST POINT, IT IS OUT OF THE QUESTION THAT I LOWER MYSELF TO MAKE PERSONAL ATTACKS.
MR PRESIDENT. IF YOU'LL PERMIT ME, I HAVE HERE A REPORT ON SOME OF COSTNER'S ACTIVITIES THAT...
I BELIEVE I WAS PERFECTLY CLEAR, MRS DALE...
15

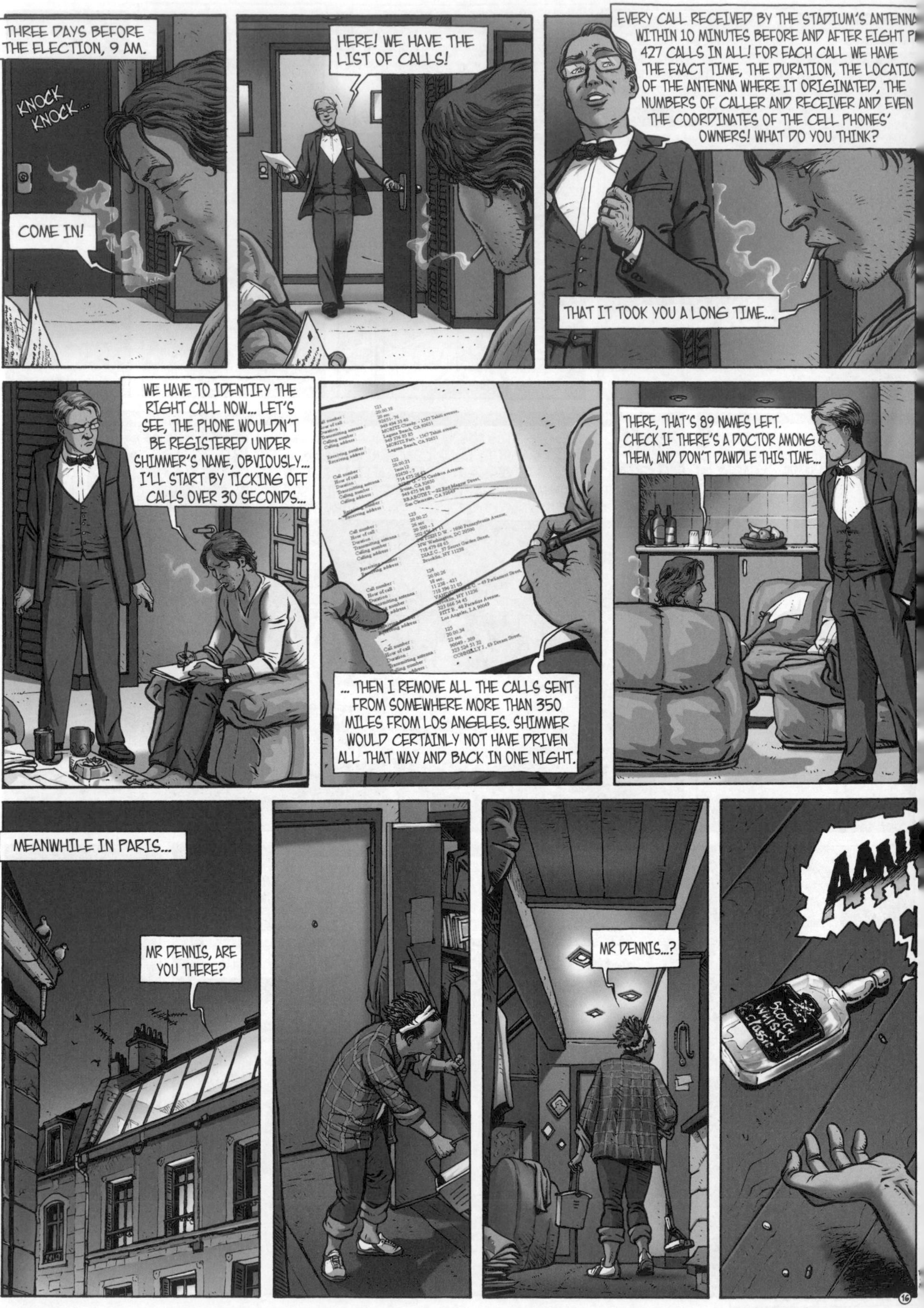
THREE DAYS BEFORE THE ELECTION, 9 AM.
KNOCK KNOCK...
COME IN!
HERE! WE HAVE THE LIST OF CALLS!
EVERY CALL RECEIVED BY THE STADIUM'S ANTENNA WITHIN 10 MINUTES BEFORE AND AFTER EIGHT P 427 CALLS IN ALL! FOR EACH CALL WE HAVE THE EXACT TIME, THE DURATION, THE LOCATIO OF THE ANTENNA WHERE IT ORIGINATED, THE NUMBERS OF CALLER AND RECEIVER AND EVEN THE COORDINATES OF THE CELL PHONES' OWNERS! WHAT DO YOU THINK?
THAT IT TOOK YOU A LONG TIME...
WE HAVE TO IDENTIFY THE RIGHT CALL NOW... LET'S SEE, THE PHONE WOULDN'T BE REGISTERED UNDER SHIMMER'S NAME, OBVIOUSLY... I'LL START BY TICKING OFF CALLS OVER 30 SECONDS...
... THEN I REMOVE ALL THE CALLS SENT FROM SOMEWHERE MORE THAN 350 MILES FROM LOS ANGELES. SHIMMER WOULD CERTAINLY NOT HAVE DRIVEN ALL THAT WAY AND BACK IN ONE NIGHT.
THERE, THAT'S 89 NAMES LEFT. CHECK IF THERE'S A DOCTOR AMONG THEM, AND DON'T DAWDLE THIS TIME...
MEANWHILE IN PARIS...
MR DENNIS, ARE YOU THERE?
MR DENNIS...?
SCOTCH WHISKY Classic
16

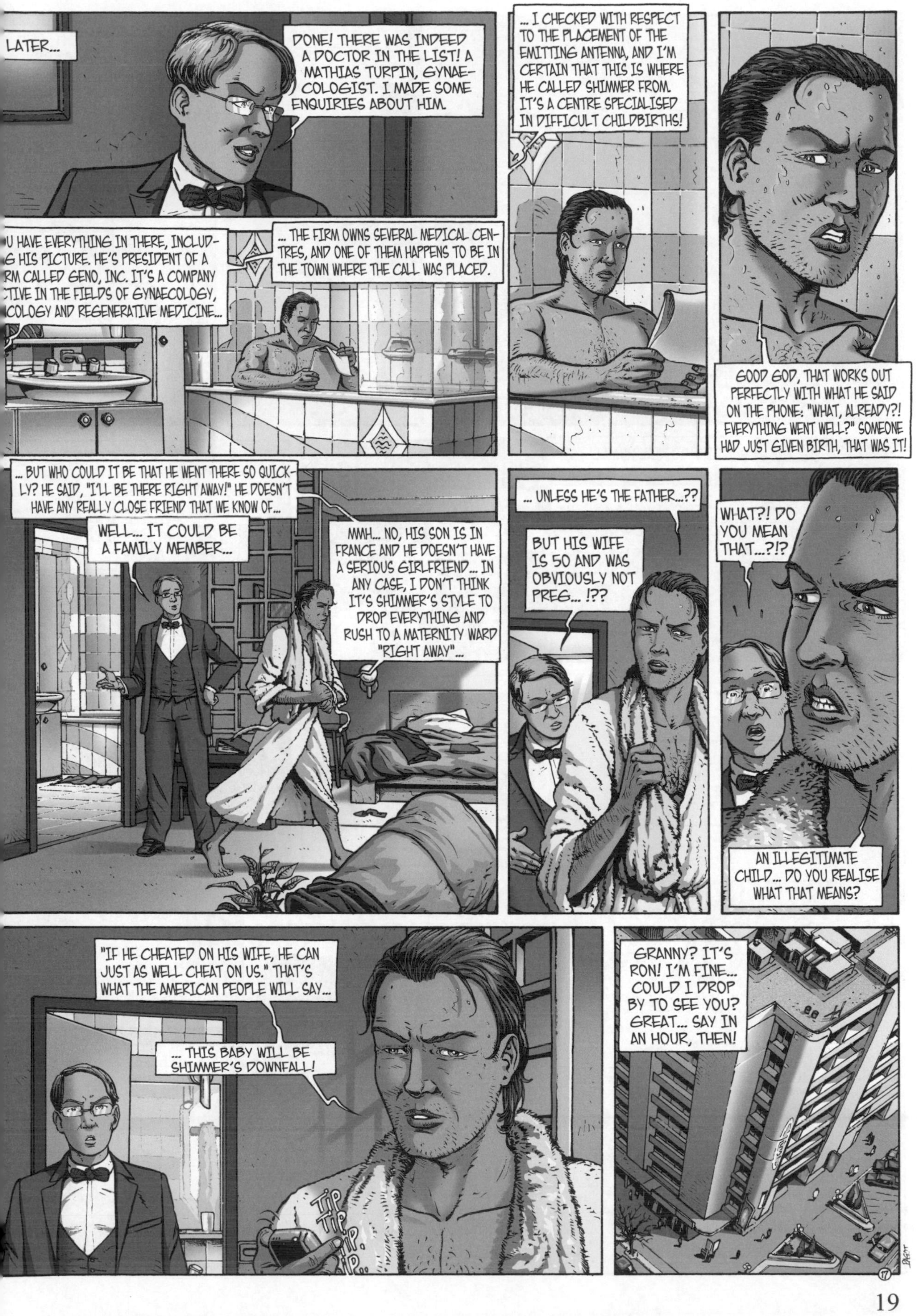
LATER...
DONE! THERE WAS INDEED A DOCTOR IN THE LIST! A MATHIAS TURPIN, GYNAE-COLOGIST. I MADE SOME ENQUIRIES ABOUT HIM.
U HAVE EVERYTHING IN THERE, INCLUD- G HIS PICTURE. HE'S PRESIDENT OF A RM CALLED GENO, INC. IT'S A COMPANY CTIVE IN THE FIELDS OF GYNAECOLOGY, COLOGY AND REGENERATIVE MEDICINE...
... THE FIRM OWNS SEVERAL MEDICAL CEN-TRES, AND ONE OF THEM HAPPENS TO BE IN THE TOWN WHERE THE CALL WAS PLACED.
... I CHECKED WITH RESPECT TO THE PLACEMENT OF THE EMITTING ANTENNA, AND I'M CERTAIN THAT THIS IS WHERE HE CALLED SHIMMER FROM. IT'S A CENTRE SPECIALISED IN DIFFICULT CHILDBIRTHS!
GOOD GOD, THAT WORKS OUT PERFECTLY WITH WHAT HE SAID ON THE PHONE: "WHAT, ALREADY?! EVERYTHING WENT WELL?" SOMEONE HAD JUST GIVEN BIRTH, THAT WAS IT!
... BUT WHO COULD IT BE THAT HE WENT THERE SO QUICK-LY? HE SAID, "I'LL BE THERE RIGHT AWAY!" HE DOESN'T HAVE ANY REALLY CLOSE FRIEND THAT WE KNOW OF...
WELL... IT COULD BE A FAMILY MEMBER...
MMH... NO, HIS SON IS IN FRANCE AND HE DOESN'T HAVE A SERIOUS GIRLFRIEND... IN ANY CASE, I DON'T THINK IT'S SHIMMER'S STYLE TO DROP EVERYTHING AND RUSH TO A MATERNITY WARD "RIGHT AWAY"...
... UNLESS HE'S THE FATHER...??
BUT HIS WIFE IS 50 AND WAS OBVIOUSLY NOT PREG... !??
WHAT?! DO YOU MEAN THAT...?!?
AN ILLEGITIMATE CHILD... DO YOU REALISE WHAT THAT MEANS?
"IF HE CHEATED ON HIS WIFE, HE CAN JUST AS WELL CHEAT ON US." THAT'S WHAT THE AMERICAN PEOPLE WILL SAY...
... THIS BABY WILL BE SHIMMER'S DOWNFALL!
TIP TIP TIP TIP...
GRANNY? IT'S RON! I'M FINE... COULD I DROP BY TO SEE YOU? GREAT... SAY IN AN HOUR, THEN!
17

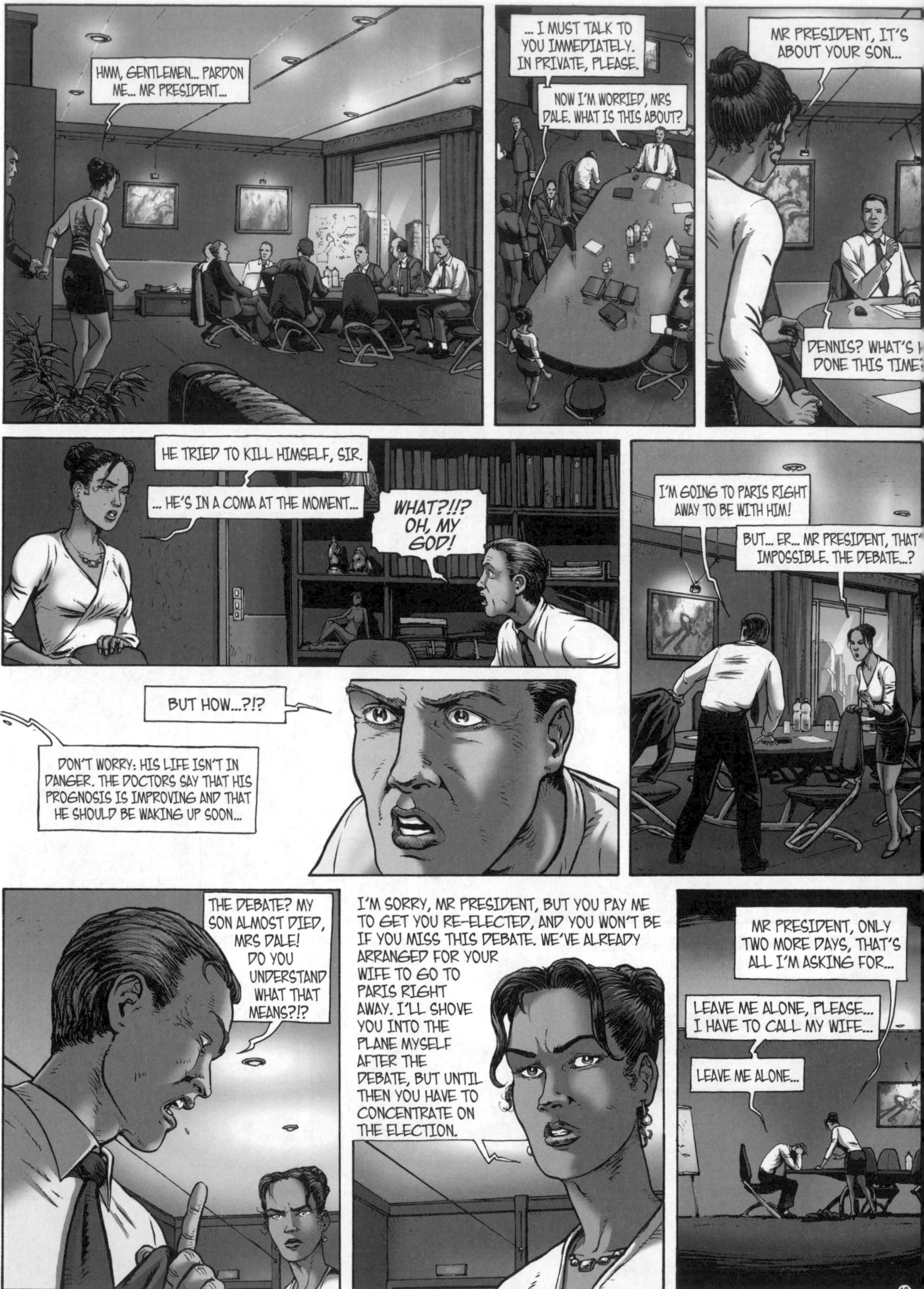

HMM, GENTLEMEN... PARDON ME... MR PRESIDENT...
... I MUST TALK TO YOU IMMEDIATELY. IN PRIVATE, PLEASE.
NOW I'M WORRIED, MRS DALE. WHAT IS THIS ABOUT?
MR PRESIDENT, IT'S ABOUT YOUR SON...
DENNIS? WHAT'S DONE THIS TIME
HE TRIED TO KILL HIMSELF, SIR.
... HE'S IN A COMA AT THE MOMENT...
WHAT?!!? OH, MY GOD!
BUT HOW...?!?
DON'T WORRY: HIS LIFE ISN'T IN DANGER. THE DOCTORS SAY THAT HIS PROGNOSIS IS IMPROVING AND THAT HE SHOULD BE WAKING UP SOON...
I'M GOING TO PARIS RIGHT AWAY TO BE WITH HIM!
BUT... ER... MR PRESIDENT, THAT' IMPOSSIBLE. THE DEBATE...?
THE DEBATE? MY SON ALMOST DIED, MRS DALE! DO YOU UNDERSTAND WHAT THAT MEANS?!?
I'M SORRY, MR PRESIDENT, BUT YOU PAY ME TO GET YOU RE-ELECTED, AND YOU WON'T BE IF YOU MISS THIS DEBATE. WE'VE ALREADY ARRANGED FOR YOUR WIFE TO GO TO PARIS RIGHT AWAY. I'LL SHOVE YOU INTO THE PLANE MYSELF AFTER THE DEBATE, BUT UNTIL THEN YOU HAVE TO CONCENTRATE ON THE ELECTION.
MR PRESIDENT, ONLY TWO MORE DAYS, THAT'S ALL I'M ASKING FOR...
LEAVE ME ALONE, PLEASE... I HAVE TO CALL MY WIFE...
LEAVE ME ALONE...
18

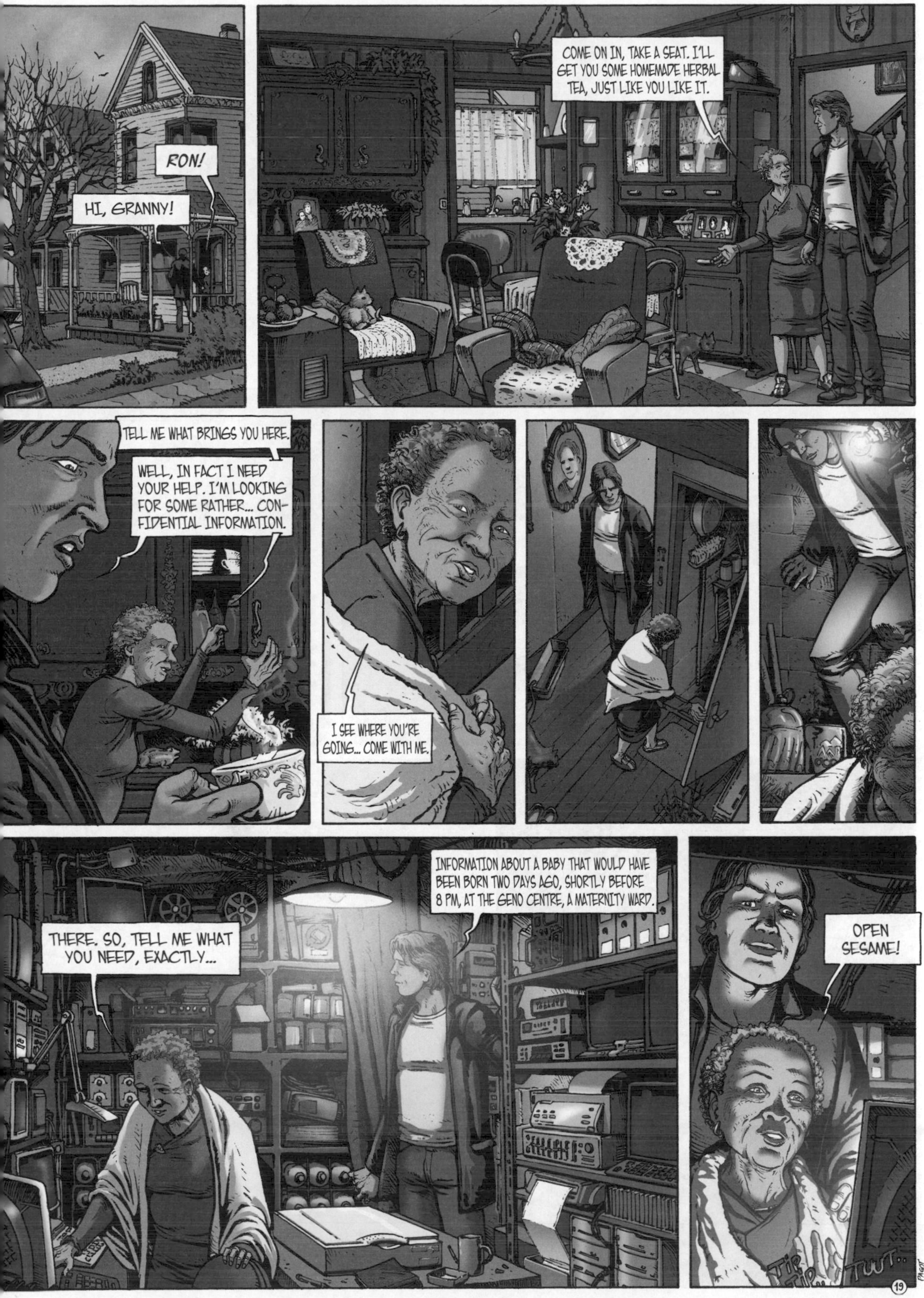
RON!
HI, GRANNY!
COME ON IN, TAKE A SEAT. I'LL GET YOU SOME HOMEMADE HERBAL TEA, JUST LIKE YOU LIKE IT.
TELL ME WHAT BRINGS YOU HERE.
WELL, IN FACT I NEED YOUR HELP. I'M LOOKING FOR SOME RATHER... CONFIDENTIAL INFORMATION.
I SEE WHERE YOU'RE GOING... COME WITH ME.
THERE. SO, TELL ME WHAT YOU NEED, EXACTLY...
INFORMATION ABOUT A BABY THAT WOULD HAVE BEEN BORN TWO DAYS AGO, SHORTLY BEFORE 8 PM, AT THE GENO CENTRE, A MATERNITY WARD.
OPEN SESAME!
TIP TIP TUUT..
19

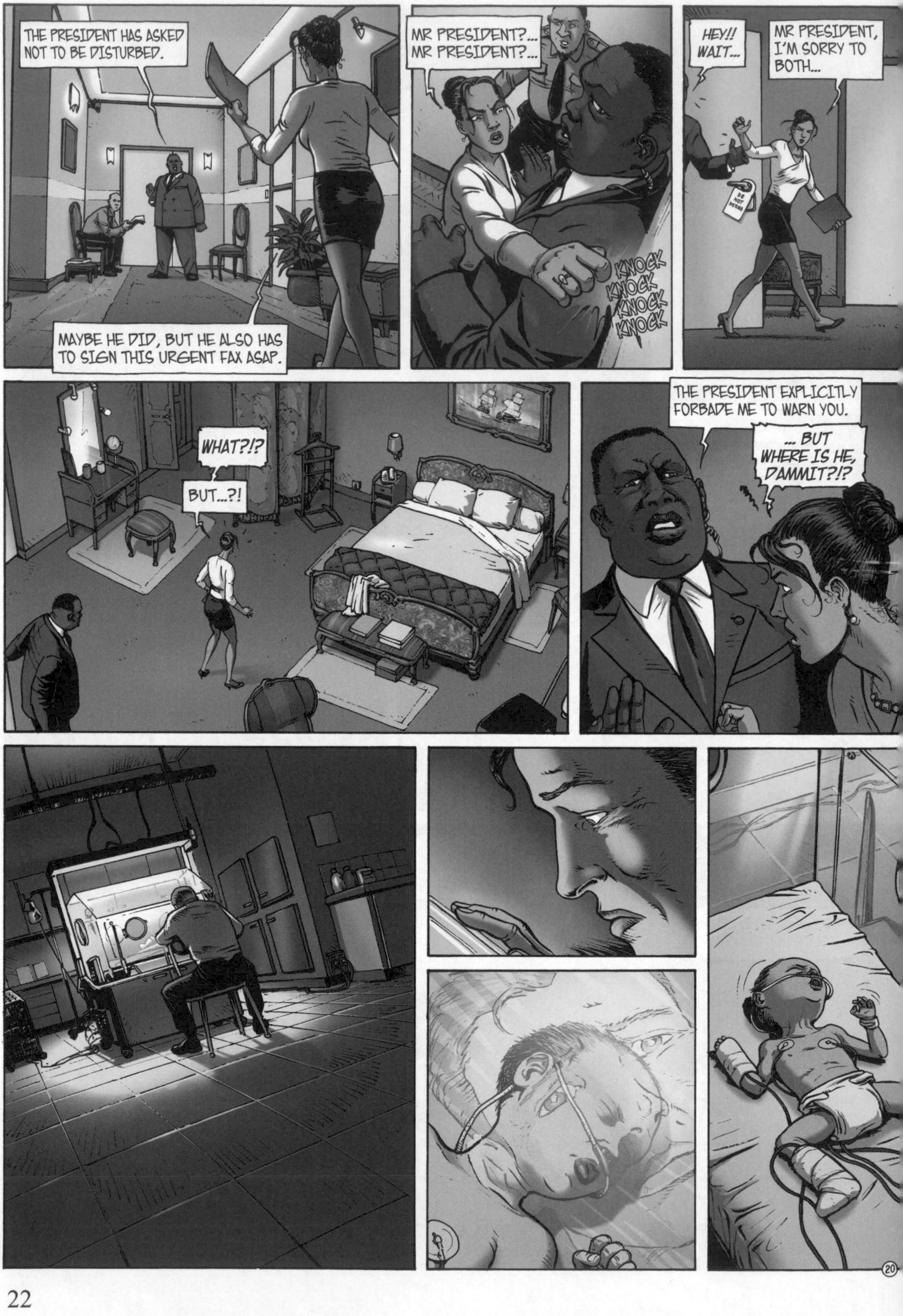
THE PRESIDENT HAS ASKED NOT TO BE DISTURBED.
MAYBE HE DID, BUT HE ALSO HAS TO SIGN THIS URGENT FAX ASAP.
MR PRESIDENT?... MR PRESIDENT?...
KNOCK KNOCK KNOCK KNOCK
HEY!! WAIT...
MR PRESIDENT, I'M SORRY TO BOTH...
DO NOT DISTURB
WHAT?!?
BUT...?!
THE PRESIDENT EXPLICITLY FORBADE ME TO WARN YOU.
... BUT WHERE IS HE, DAMMIT?!?
20

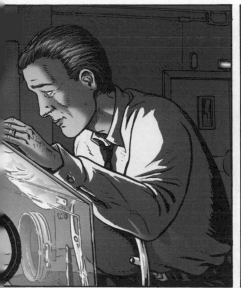

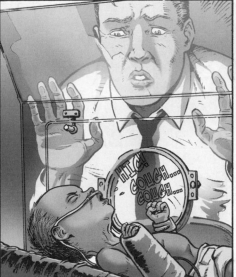

HIC! COUGH... COUGH...

DZZZ...

AHEM...

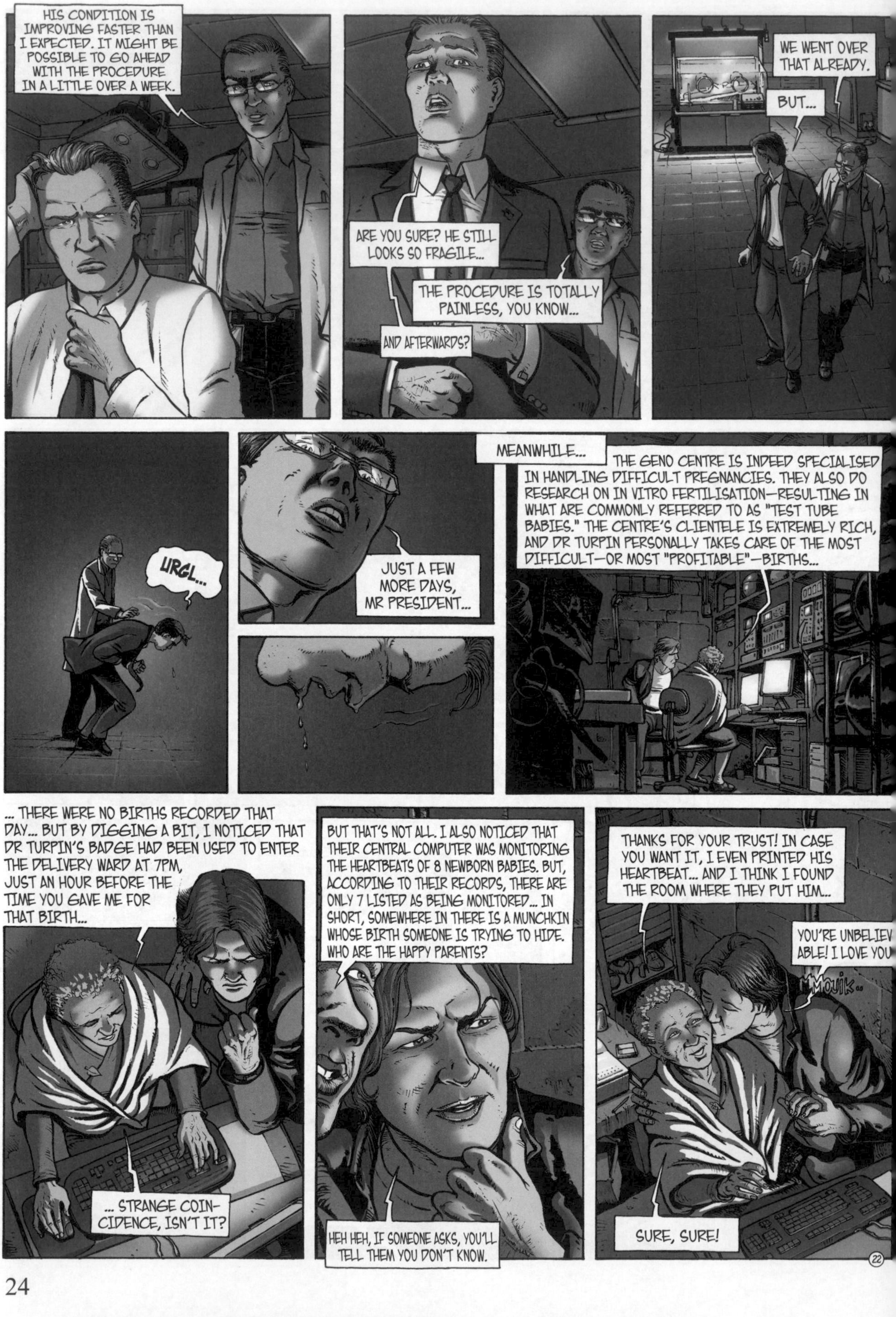
HIS CONDITION IS IMPROVING FASTER THAN I EXPECTED. IT MIGHT BE POSSIBLE TO GO AHEAD WITH THE PROCEDURE IN A LITTLE OVER A WEEK.
ARE YOU SURE? HE STILL LOOKS SO FRAGILE...
THE PROCEDURE IS TOTALLY PAINLESS, YOU KNOW...
AND AFTERWARDS?
WE WENT OVER THAT ALREADY.
BUT...
URGL...
JUST A FEW MORE DAYS, MR PRESIDENT...
MEANWHILE...
THE GENO CENTRE IS INDEED SPECIALISED IN HANDLING DIFFICULT PREGNANCIES. THEY ALSO DO RESEARCH ON IN VITRO FERTILISATION—RESULTING IN WHAT ARE COMMONLY REFERRED TO AS "TEST TUBE BABIES." THE CENTRE'S CLIENTELE IS EXTREMELY RICH, AND DR TURPIN PERSONALLY TAKES CARE OF THE MOST DIFFICULT—OR MOST "PROFITABLE"—BIRTHS...
... THERE WERE NO BIRTHS RECORDED THAT DAY... BUT BY DIGGING A BIT, I NOTICED THAT DR TURPIN'S BADGE HAD BEEN USED TO ENTER THE DELIVERY WARD AT 7PM, JUST AN HOUR BEFORE THE TIME YOU GAVE ME FOR THAT BIRTH...
... STRANGE COINCIDENCE, ISN'T IT?
BUT THAT'S NOT ALL. I ALSO NOTICED THAT THEIR CENTRAL COMPUTER WAS MONITORING THE HEARTBEATS OF 8 NEWBORN BABIES. BUT, ACCORDING TO THEIR RECORDS, THERE ARE ONLY 7 LISTED AS BEING MONITORED... IN SHORT, SOMEWHERE IN THERE IS A MUNCHKIN WHOSE BIRTH SOMEONE IS TRYING TO HIDE. WHO ARE THE HAPPY PARENTS?
HEH HEH, IF SOMEONE ASKS, YOU'LL TELL THEM YOU DON'T KNOW.
THANKS FOR YOUR TRUST! IN CASE YOU WANT IT, I EVEN PRINTED HIS HEARTBEAT... AND I THINK I FOUND THE ROOM WHERE THEY PUT HIM...
YOU'RE UNBELIEV ABLE! I LOVE YOU
MMOUIK..
SURE, SURE!
22

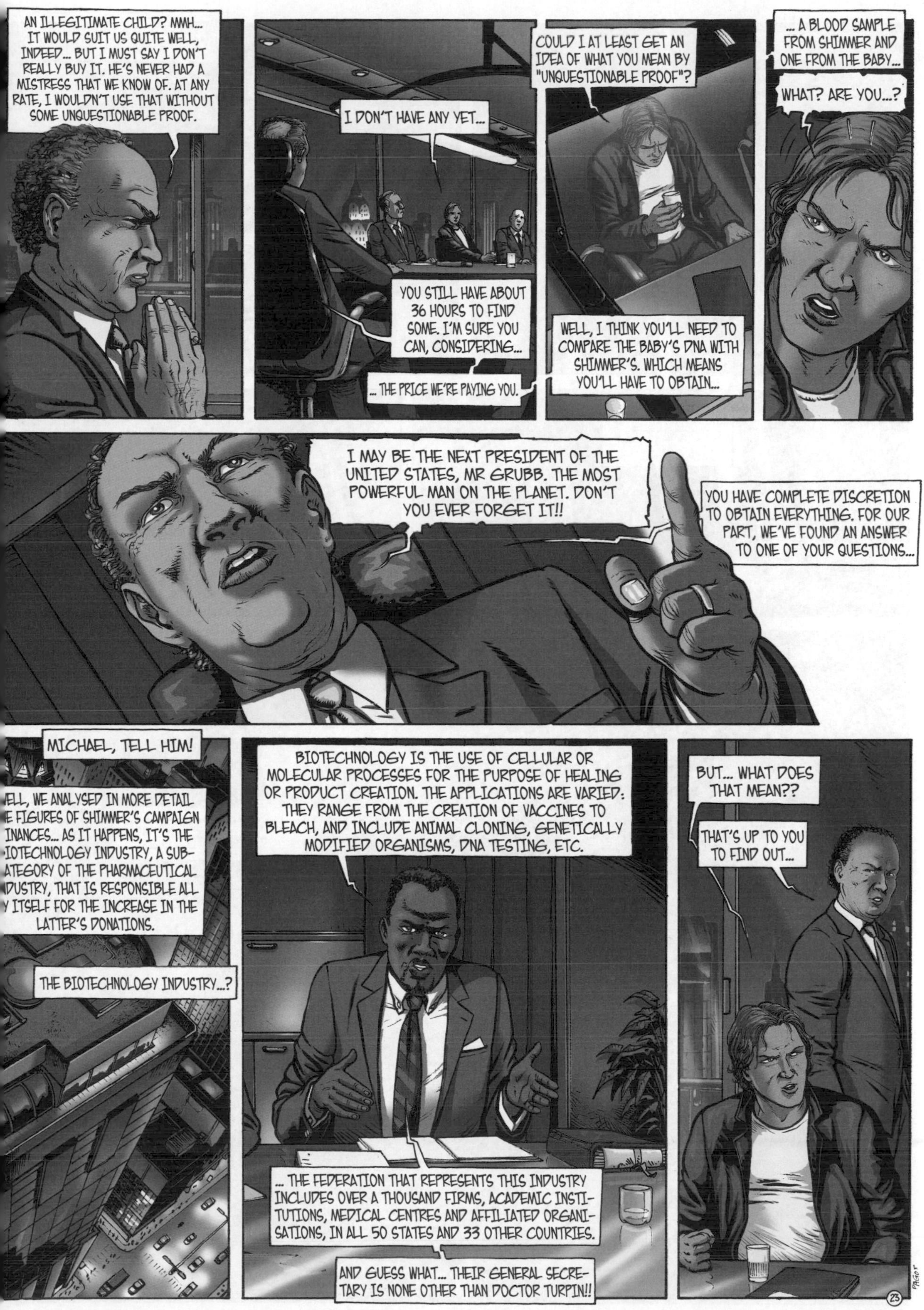
AN ILLEGITIMATE CHILD? MMH... IT WOULD SUIT US QUITE WELL, INDEED... BUT I MUST SAY I DON'T REALLY BUY IT. HE'S NEVER HAD A MISTRESS THAT WE KNOW OF. AT ANY RATE, I WOULDN'T USE THAT WITHOUT SOME UNQUESTIONABLE PROOF.
I DON'T HAVE ANY YET...
YOU STILL HAVE ABOUT 36 HOURS TO FIND SOME. I'M SURE YOU CAN, CONSIDERING...
... THE PRICE WE'RE PAYING YOU.
COULD I AT LEAST GET AN IDEA OF WHAT YOU MEAN BY "UNQUESTIONABLE PROOF"?
WELL, I THINK YOU'LL NEED TO COMPARE THE BABY'S DNA WITH SHIMMER'S. WHICH MEANS YOU'LL HAVE TO OBTAIN...
... A BLOOD SAMPLE FROM SHIMMER AND ONE FROM THE BABY...
WHAT? ARE YOU...?
I MAY BE THE NEXT PRESIDENT OF THE UNITED STATES, MR GRUBB. THE MOST POWERFUL MAN ON THE PLANET. DON'T YOU EVER FORGET IT!!
YOU HAVE COMPLETE DISCRETION TO OBTAIN EVERYTHING. FOR OUR PART, WE'VE FOUND AN ANSWER TO ONE OF YOUR QUESTIONS...
MICHAEL, TELL HIM!
ELL, WE ANALYSED IN MORE DETAIL E FIGURES OF SHIMMER'S CAMPAIGN INANCES... AS IT HAPPENS, IT'S THE IOTECHNOLOGY INDUSTRY, A SUB-ATEGORY OF THE PHARMACEUTICAL NDUSTRY, THAT IS RESPONSIBLE ALL Y ITSELF FOR THE INCREASE IN THE LATTER'S DONATIONS.
THE BIOTECHNOLOGY INDUSTRY...?
BIOTECHNOLOGY IS THE USE OF CELLULAR OR MOLECULAR PROCESSES FOR THE PURPOSE OF HEALING OR PRODUCT CREATION. THE APPLICATIONS ARE VARIED: THEY RANGE FROM THE CREATION OF VACCINES TO BLEACH, AND INCLUDE ANIMAL CLONING, GENETICALLY MODIFIED ORGANISMS, DNA TESTING, ETC.
... THE FEDERATION THAT REPRESENTS THIS INDUSTRY INCLUDES OVER A THOUSAND FIRMS, ACADEMIC INSTITUTIONS, MEDICAL CENTRES AND AFFILIATED ORGANISATIONS, IN ALL 50 STATES AND 33 OTHER COUNTRIES.
AND GUESS WHAT... THEIR GENERAL SECRETARY IS NONE OTHER THAN DOCTOR TURPIN!!
BUT... WHAT DOES THAT MEAN??
THAT'S UP TO YOU TO FIND OUT...
23

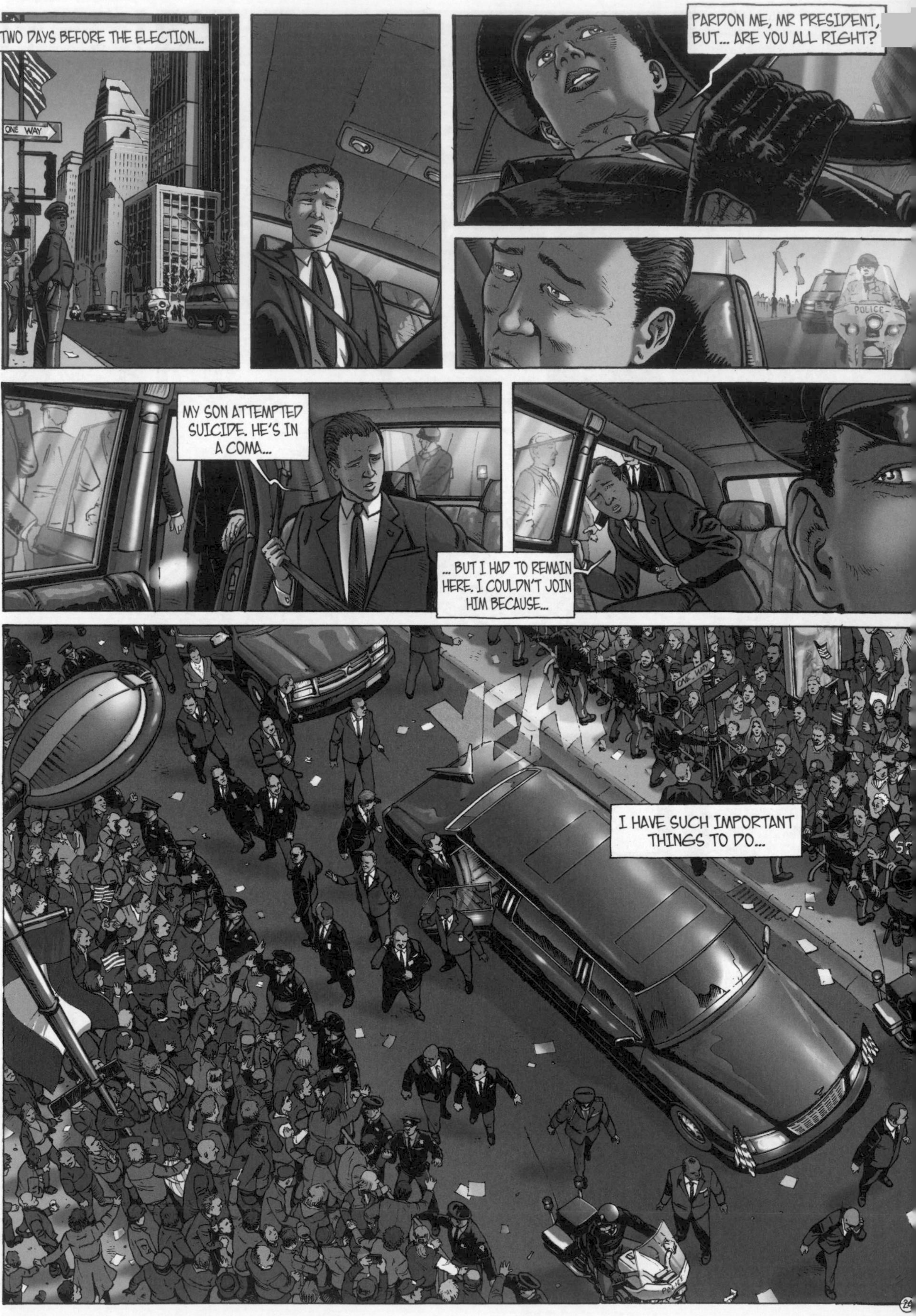
TWO DAYS BEFORE THE ELECTION...
PARDON ME, MR PRESIDENT, BUT... ARE YOU ALL RIGHT?
MY SON ATTEMPTED SUICIDE. HE'S IN A COMA...
... BUT I HAD TO REMAIN HERE. I COULDN'T JOIN HIM BECAUSE...
I HAVE SUCH IMPORTANT THINGS TO DO...

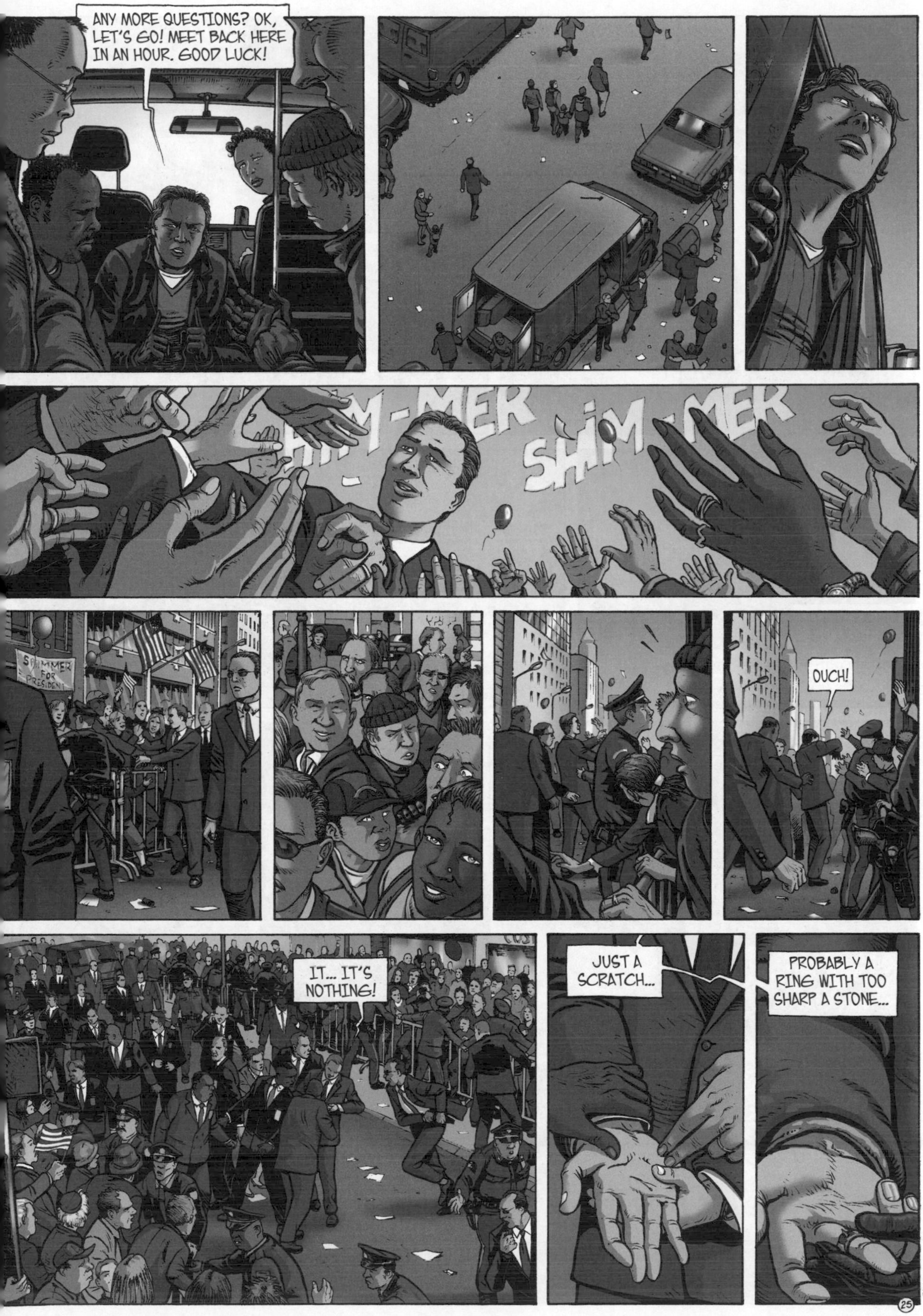
ANY MORE QUESTIONS? OK, LET'S GO! MEET BACK HERE IN AN HOUR. GOOD LUCK!
SHIM-MER SHIM-MER
SHIMMER FOR PRESIDENT
OUCH!
IT... IT'S NOTHING!
JUST A SCRATCH...
PROBABLY A RING WITH TOO SHARP A STONE...
25
PAGOT

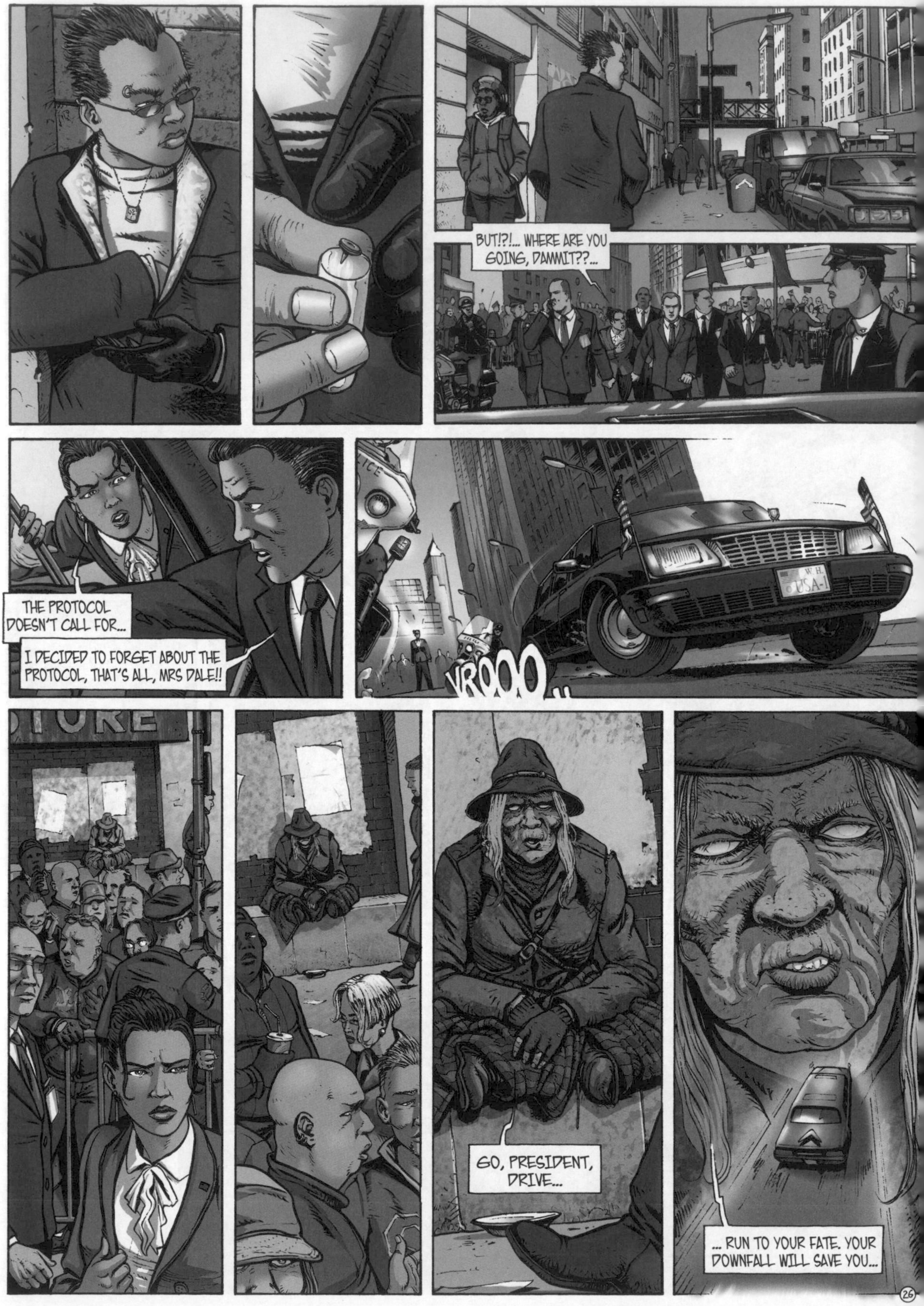
BUT!?!... WHERE ARE YOU GOING, DAMMIT??...
THE PROTOCOL DOESN'T CALL FOR...
I DECIDED TO FORGET ABOUT THE PROTOCOL, THAT'S ALL, MRS DALE!!
W.H.
USA-1
VROOO...
GO, PRESIDENT, DRIVE...
... RUN TO YOUR FATE. YOUR DOWNFALL WILL SAVE YOU...
26

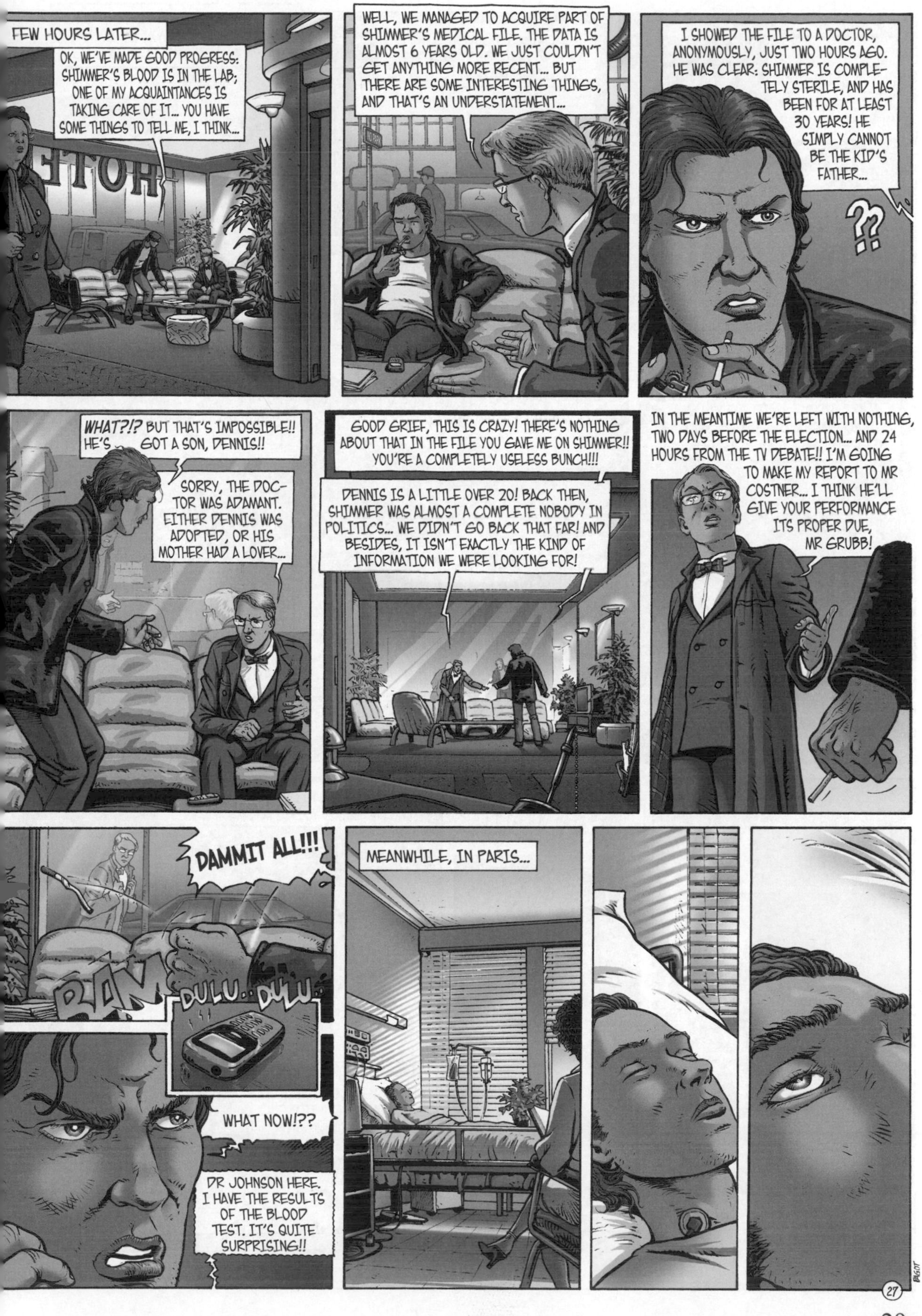
FEW HOURS LATER...
OK, WE'VE MADE GOOD PROGRESS: SHIMMER'S BLOOD IS IN THE LAB; ONE OF MY ACQUAINTANCES IS TAKING CARE OF IT... YOU HAVE SOME THINGS TO TELL ME, I THINK...
HOTEL
WELL, WE MANAGED TO ACQUIRE PART OF SHIMMER'S MEDICAL FILE. THE DATA IS ALMOST 6 YEARS OLD. WE JUST COULDN'T GET ANYTHING MORE RECENT... BUT THERE ARE SOME INTERESTING THINGS, AND THAT'S AN UNDERSTATEMENT...
I SHOWED THE FILE TO A DOCTOR, ANONYMOUSLY, JUST TWO HOURS AGO. HE WAS CLEAR: SHIMMER IS COMPLETELY STERILE, AND HAS BEEN FOR AT LEAST 30 YEARS! HE SIMPLY CANNOT BE THE KID'S FATHER...
??
WHAT?!? BUT THAT'S IMPOSSIBLE!! HE'S GOT A SON, DENNIS!!
SORRY, THE DOCTOR WAS ADAMANT. EITHER DENNIS WAS ADOPTED, OR HIS MOTHER HAD A LOVER...
GOOD GRIEF, THIS IS CRAZY! THERE'S NOTHING ABOUT THAT IN THE FILE YOU GAVE ME ON SHIMMER!! YOU'RE A COMPLETELY USELESS BUNCH!!!
DENNIS IS A LITTLE OVER 20! BACK THEN, SHIMMER WAS ALMOST A COMPLETE NOBODY IN POLITICS... WE DIDN'T GO BACK THAT FAR! AND BESIDES, IT ISN'T EXACTLY THE KIND OF INFORMATION WE WERE LOOKING FOR!
IN THE MEANTIME WE'RE LEFT WITH NOTHING, TWO DAYS BEFORE THE ELECTION... AND 24 HOURS FROM THE TV DEBATE!! I'M GOING TO MAKE MY REPORT TO MR COSTNER... I THINK HE'LL GIVE YOUR PERFORMANCE ITS PROPER DUE, MR GRUBB!
DAMMIT ALL!!!
BAM
DULU.. DULU..
WHAT NOW!??
DR JOHNSON HERE. I HAVE THE RESULTS OF THE BLOOD TEST. IT'S QUITE SURPRISING!!
MEANWHILE, IN PARIS...
27

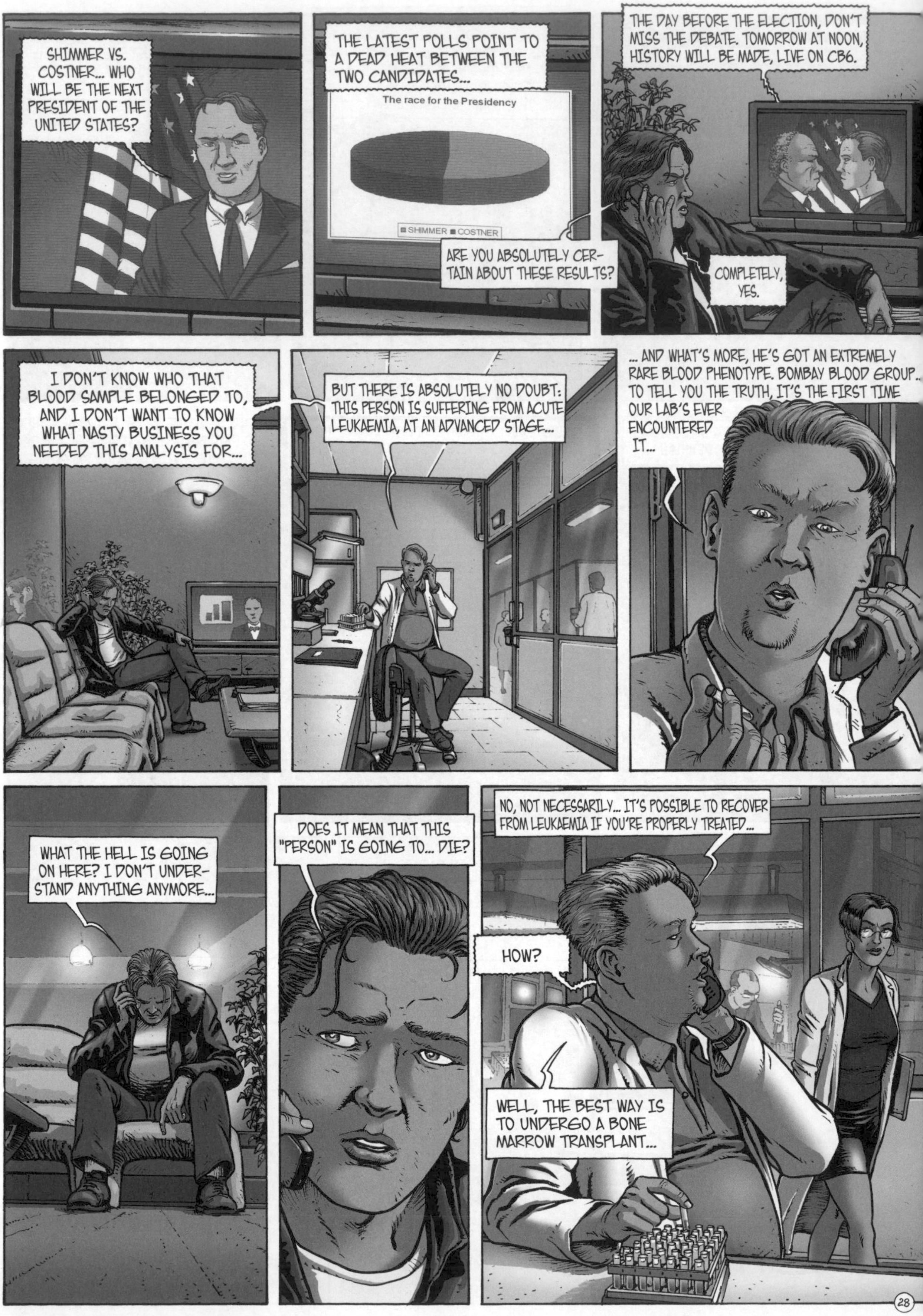
SHIMMER VS. COSTNER... WHO WILL BE THE NEXT PRESIDENT OF THE UNITED STATES?
THE LATEST POLLS POINT TO A DEAD HEAT BETWEEN THE TWO CANDIDATES...
The race for the Presidency
SHIMMER
COSTNER
ARE YOU ABSOLUTELY CER-TAIN ABOUT THESE RESULTS?
THE DAY BEFORE THE ELECTION, DON'T MISS THE DEBATE. TOMORROW AT NOON, HISTORY WILL BE MADE, LIVE ON CB6.
COMPLETELY, YES.
I DON'T KNOW WHO THAT BLOOD SAMPLE BELONGED TO, AND I DON'T WANT TO KNOW WHAT NASTY BUSINESS YOU NEEDED THIS ANALYSIS FOR...
BUT THERE IS ABSOLUTELY NO DOUBT: THIS PERSON IS SUFFERING FROM ACUTE LEUKAEMIA, AT AN ADVANCED STAGE...
... AND WHAT'S MORE, HE'S GOT AN EXTREMELY RARE BLOOD PHENOTYPE. BOMBAY BLOOD GROUP... TO TELL YOU THE TRUTH, IT'S THE FIRST TIME OUR LAB'S EVER ENCOUNTERED IT...
WHAT THE HELL IS GOING ON HERE? I DON'T UNDER-STAND ANYTHING ANYMORE...
DOES IT MEAN THAT THIS "PERSON" IS GOING TO... DIE?
NO, NOT NECESSARILY... IT'S POSSIBLE TO RECOVER FROM LEUKAEMIA IF YOU'RE PROPERLY TREATED...
HOW?
WELL, THE BEST WAY IS TO UNDERGO A BONE MARROW TRANSPLANT...
28

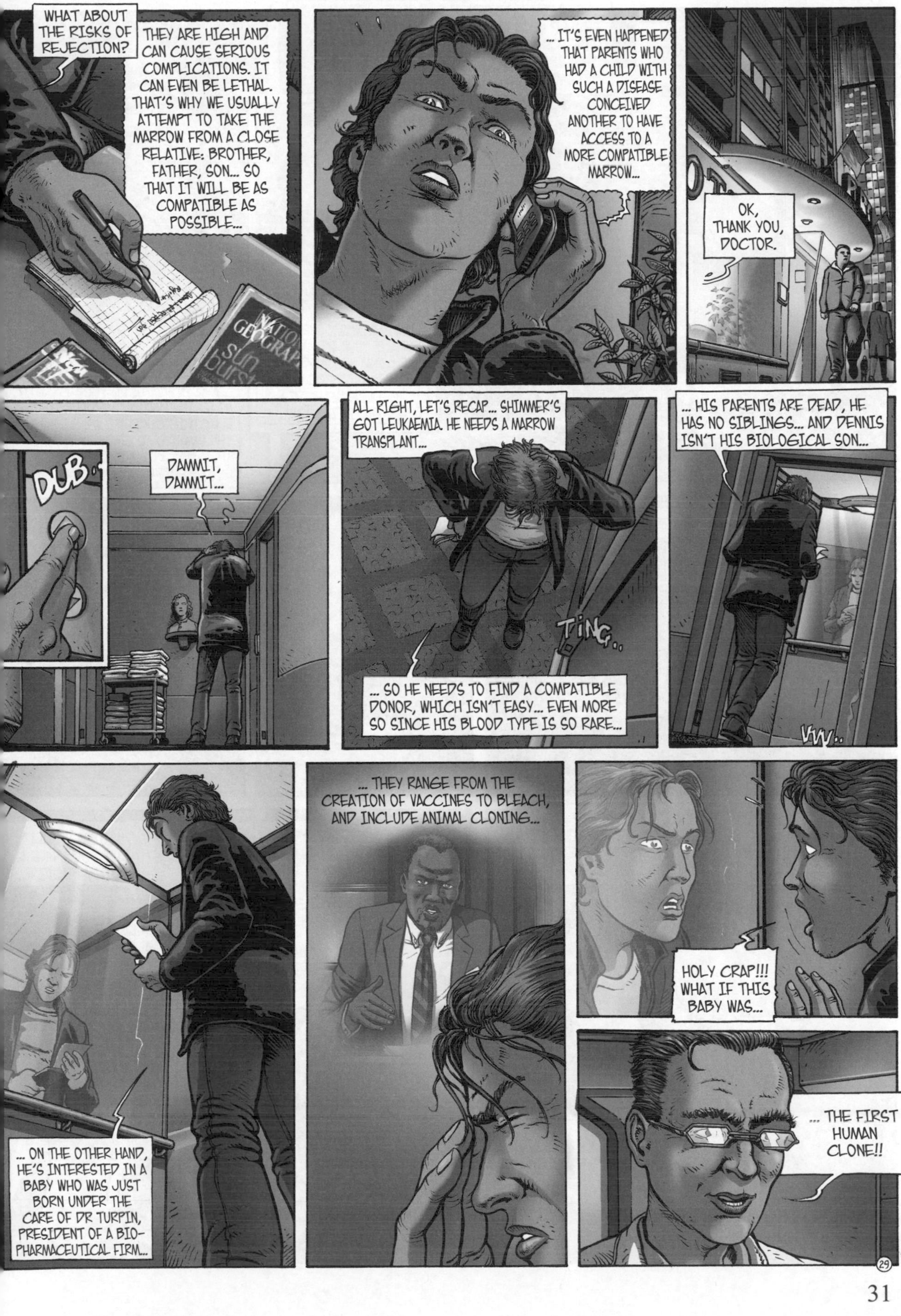

WHAT ABOUT THE RISKS OF REJECTION?
THEY ARE HIGH AND CAN CAUSE SERIOUS COMPLICATIONS. IT CAN EVEN BE LETHAL. THAT'S WHY WE USUALLY ATTEMPT TO TAKE THE MARROW FROM A CLOSE RELATIVE: BROTHER, FATHER, SON... SO THAT IT WILL BE AS COMPATIBLE AS POSSIBLE...
... IT'S EVEN HAPPENED THAT PARENTS WHO HAD A CHILD WITH SUCH A DISEASE CONCEIVED ANOTHER TO HAVE ACCESS TO A MORE COMPATIBLE MARROW...
OK, THANK YOU, DOCTOR.
DUB
DAMMIT, DAMMIT...
ALL RIGHT, LET'S RECAP... SHIMMER'S GOT LEUKAEMIA. HE NEEDS A MARROW TRANSPLANT...
TING..
... SO HE NEEDS TO FIND A COMPATIBLE DONOR, WHICH ISN'T EASY... EVEN MORE SO SINCE HIS BLOOD TYPE IS SO RARE...
... HIS PARENTS ARE DEAD, HE HAS NO SIBLINGS... AND DENNIS ISN'T HIS BIOLOGICAL SON...
VVV..
... ON THE OTHER HAND, HE'S INTERESTED IN A BABY WHO WAS JUST BORN UNDER THE CARE OF DR TURPIN, PRESIDENT OF A BIO-PHARMACEUTICAL FIRM...
... THEY RANGE FROM THE CREATION OF VACCINES TO BLEACH, AND INCLUDE ANIMAL CLONING...
HOLY CRAP!!! WHAT IF THIS BABY WAS...
... THE FIRST HUMAN CLONE!!
PAGOT
29

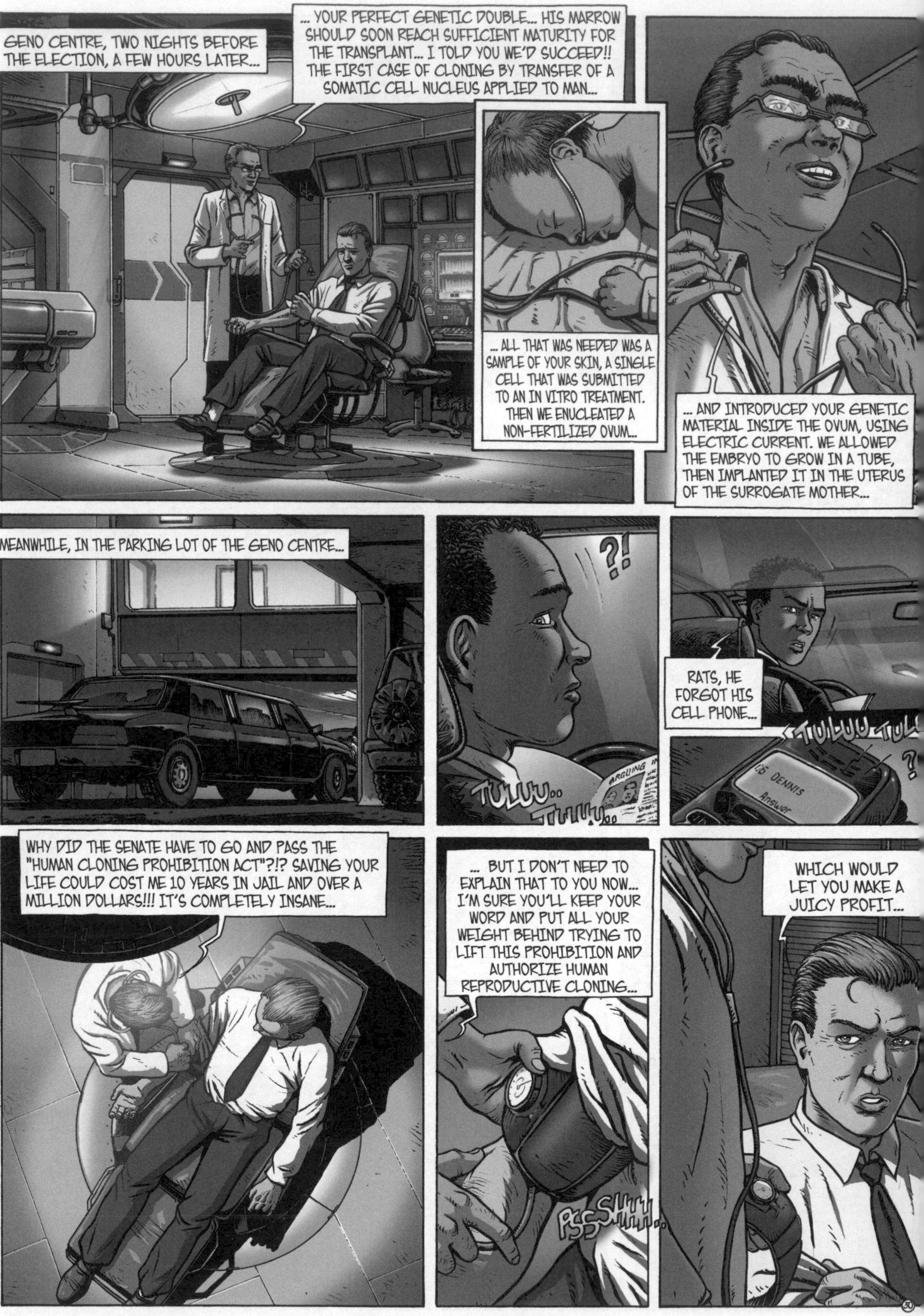
GENO CENTRE, TWO NIGHTS BEFORE THE ELECTION, A FEW HOURS LATER...
... YOUR PERFECT GENETIC DOUBLE... HIS MARROW SHOULD SOON REACH SUFFICIENT MATURITY FOR THE TRANSPLANT... I TOLD YOU WE'D SUCCEED!! THE FIRST CASE OF CLONING BY TRANSFER OF A SOMATIC CELL NUCLEUS APPLIED TO MAN...
... ALL THAT WAS NEEDED WAS A SAMPLE OF YOUR SKIN, A SINGLE CELL THAT WAS SUBMITTED TO AN IN VITRO TREATMENT. THEN WE ENUCLEATED A NON-FERTILIZED OVUM...
... AND INTRODUCED YOUR GENETIC MATERIAL INSIDE THE OVUM, USING ELECTRIC CURRENT. WE ALLOWED THE EMBRYO TO GROW IN A TUBE, THEN IMPLANTED IT IN THE UTERUS OF THE SURROGATE MOTHER...
MEANWHILE, IN THE PARKING LOT OF THE GENO CENTRE...
?!
TULUU..
TULUU..
RATS, HE FORGOT HIS CELL PHONE...
TULUU TUL
?
WHY DID THE SENATE HAVE TO GO AND PASS THE "HUMAN CLONING PROHIBITION ACT"?!? SAVING YOUR LIFE COULD COST ME 10 YEARS IN JAIL AND OVER A MILLION DOLLARS!!! IT'S COMPLETELY INSANE...
... BUT I DON'T NEED TO EXPLAIN THAT TO YOU NOW... I'M SURE YOU'LL KEEP YOUR WORD AND PUT ALL YOUR WEIGHT BEHIND TRYING TO LIFT THIS PROHIBITION AND AUTHORIZE HUMAN REPRODUCTIVE CLONING...
PSSSHHH..
WHICH WOULD LET YOU MAKE A JUICY PROFIT...

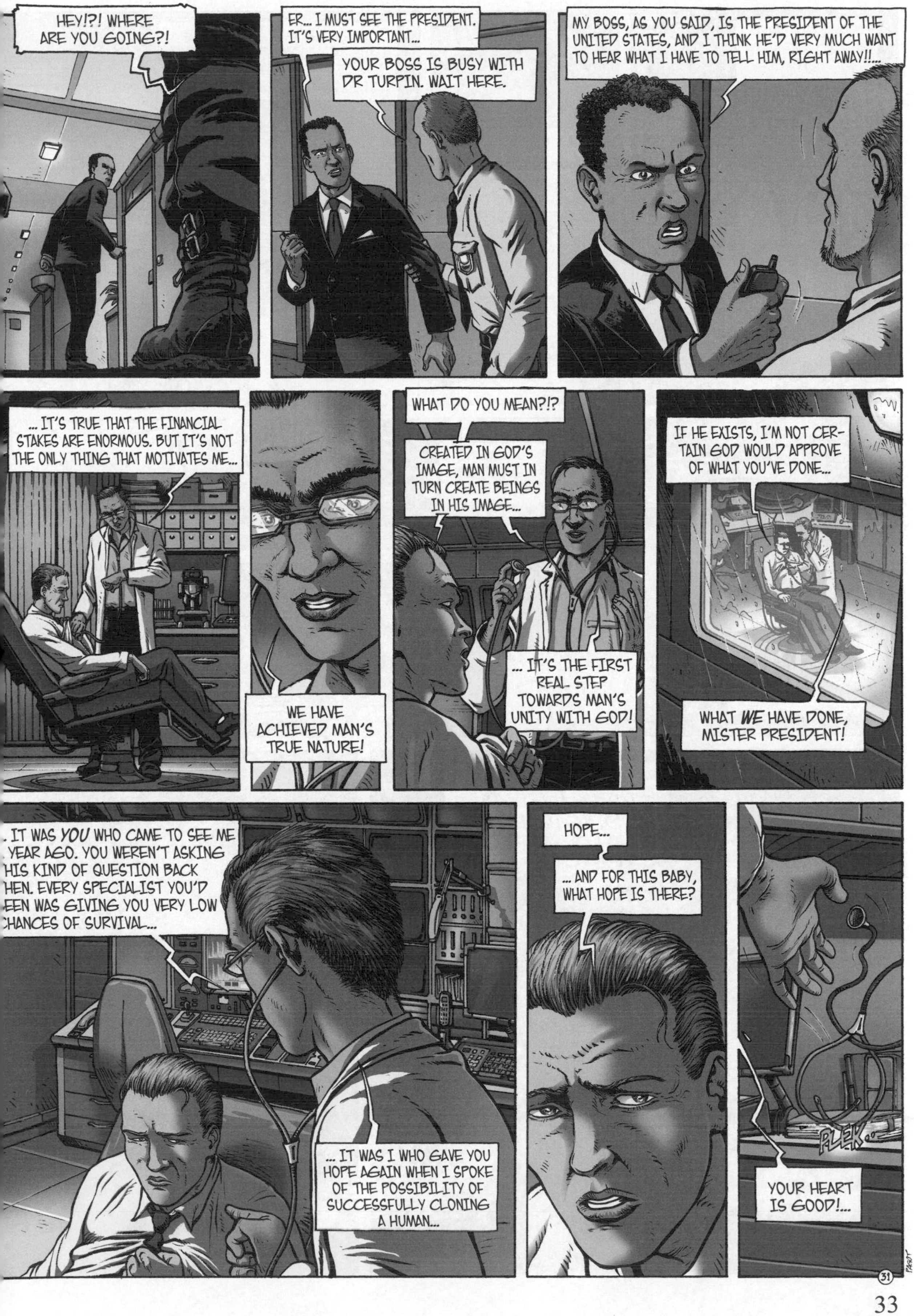
HEY!?! WHERE ARE YOU GOING?!
ER... I MUST SEE THE PRESIDENT. IT'S VERY IMPORTANT...
YOUR BOSS IS BUSY WITH DR TURPIN. WAIT HERE.
MY BOSS, AS YOU SAID, IS THE PRESIDENT OF THE UNITED STATES, AND I THINK HE'D VERY MUCH WANT TO HEAR WHAT I HAVE TO TELL HIM, RIGHT AWAY!!...
... IT'S TRUE THAT THE FINANCIAL STAKES ARE ENORMOUS. BUT IT'S NOT THE ONLY THING THAT MOTIVATES ME...
WE HAVE ACHIEVED MAN'S TRUE NATURE!
WHAT DO YOU MEAN?!?
CREATED IN GOD'S IMAGE, MAN MUST IN TURN CREATE BEINGS IN HIS IMAGE...
... IT'S THE FIRST REAL STEP TOWARDS MAN'S UNITY WITH GOD!
IF HE EXISTS, I'M NOT CERTAIN GOD WOULD APPROVE OF WHAT YOU'VE DONE...
WHAT WE HAVE DONE, MISTER PRESIDENT!
. IT WAS YOU WHO CAME TO SEE ME YEAR AGO. YOU WEREN'T ASKING HIS KIND OF QUESTION BACK HEN. EVERY SPECIALIST YOU'D EEN WAS GIVING YOU VERY LOW CHANCES OF SURVIVAL...
... IT WAS I WHO GAVE YOU HOPE AGAIN WHEN I SPOKE OF THE POSSIBILITY OF SUCCESSFULLY CLONING A HUMAN...
HOPE...
... AND FOR THIS BABY, WHAT HOPE IS THERE?
PLEK..
YOUR HEART IS GOOD!...
31

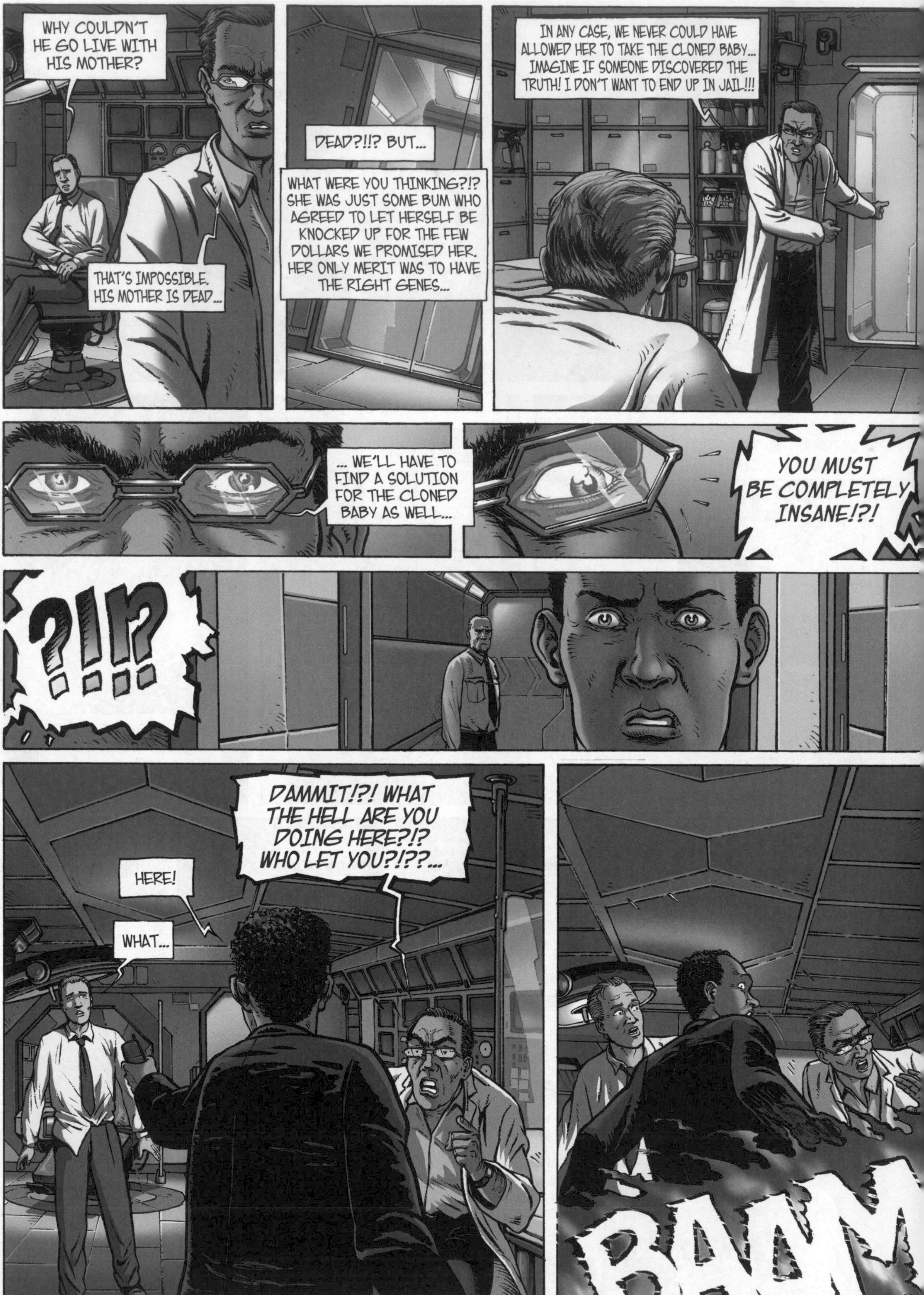
WHY COULDN'T HE GO LIVE WITH HIS MOTHER?
THAT'S IMPOSSIBLE. HIS MOTHER IS DEAD...
DEAD?!!? BUT...
WHAT WERE YOU THINKING?!? SHE WAS JUST SOME BUM WHO AGREED TO LET HERSELF BE KNOCKED UP FOR THE FEW DOLLARS WE PROMISED HER. HER ONLY MERIT WAS TO HAVE THE RIGHT GENES...
IN ANY CASE, WE NEVER COULD HAVE ALLOWED HER TO TAKE THE CLONED BABY... IMAGINE IF SOMEONE DISCOVERED THE TRUTH! I DON'T WANT TO END UP IN JAIL!!!
... WE'LL HAVE TO FIND A SOLUTION FOR THE CLONED BABY AS WELL...
YOU MUST BE COMPLETELY INSANE!?!
?!!?
HERE!
WHAT...
DAMMIT!?! WHAT THE HELL ARE YOU DOING HERE?!? WHO LET YOU?!??...
BAAM
PAGOT
32

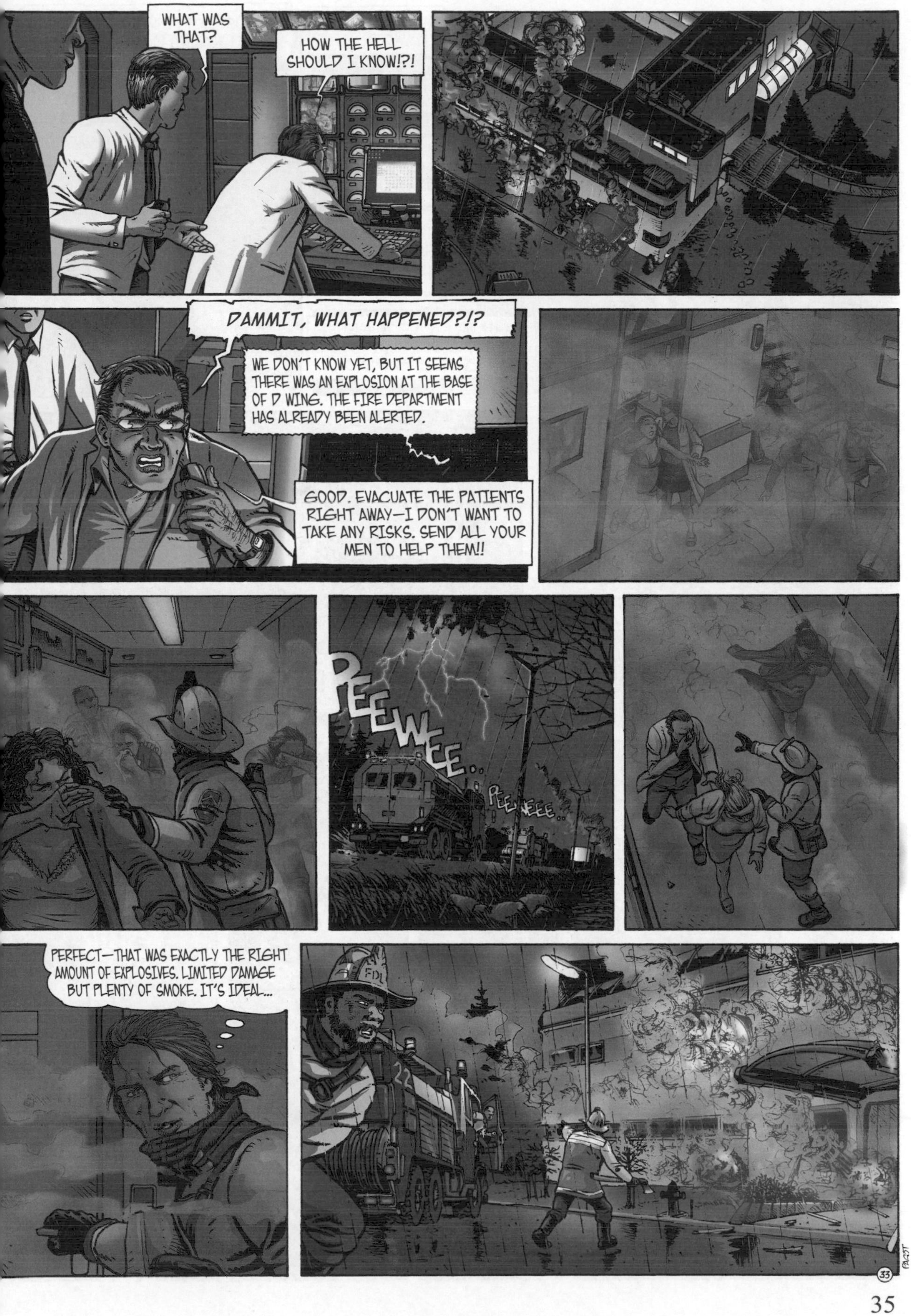
WHAT WAS THAT?
HOW THE HELL SHOULD I KNOW!?!
DAMMIT, WHAT HAPPENED?!?
WE DON'T KNOW YET, BUT IT SEEMS THERE WAS AN EXPLOSION AT THE BASE OF D WING. THE FIRE DEPARTMENT HAS ALREADY BEEN ALERTED.
GOOD. EVACUATE THE PATIENTS RIGHT AWAY—I DON'T WANT TO TAKE ANY RISKS. SEND ALL YOUR MEN TO HELP THEM!!
PEEWEEE..
PEEWEEE..
PERFECT—THAT WAS EXACTLY THE RIGHT AMOUNT OF EXPLOSIVES. LIMITED DAMAGE BUT PLENTY OF SMOKE. IT'S IDEAL...
FDI
22
33

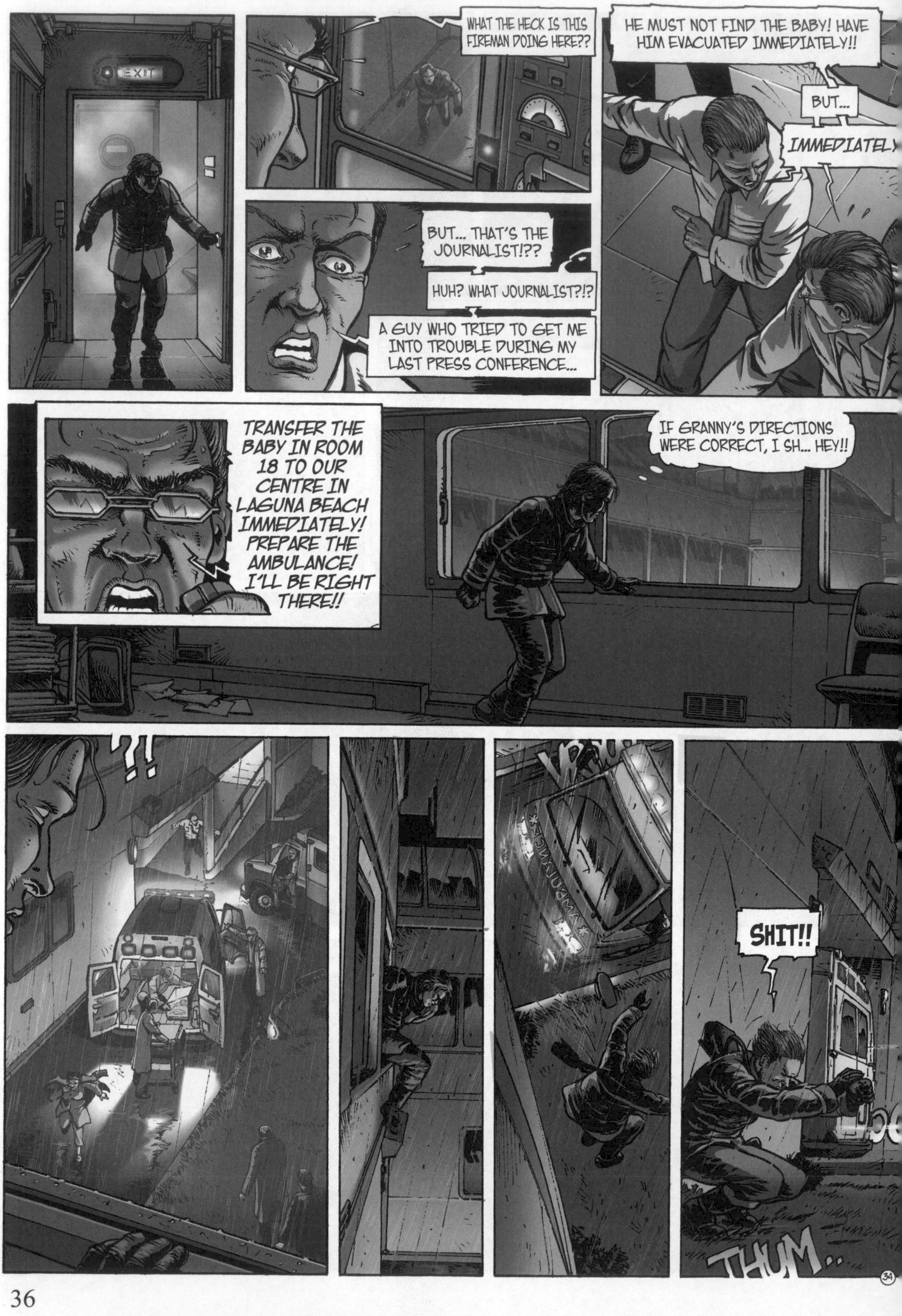
EXIT
WHAT THE HECK IS THIS FIREMAN DOING HERE??
HE MUST NOT FIND THE BABY! HAVE HIM EVACUATED IMMEDIATELY!!
BUT...
IMMEDIATEL
BUT... THAT'S THE JOURNALIST!??
HUH? WHAT JOURNALIST?!?
A GUY WHO TRIED TO GET ME INTO TROUBLE DURING MY LAST PRESS CONFERENCE...
TRANSFER THE BABY IN ROOM 18 TO OUR CENTRE IN LAGUNA BEACH IMMEDIATELY! PREPARE THE AMBULANCE! I'LL BE RIGHT THERE!!
IF GRANNY'S DIRECTIONS WERE CORRECT, I SH... HEY!!
?!
SHIT!!
THUM..
34

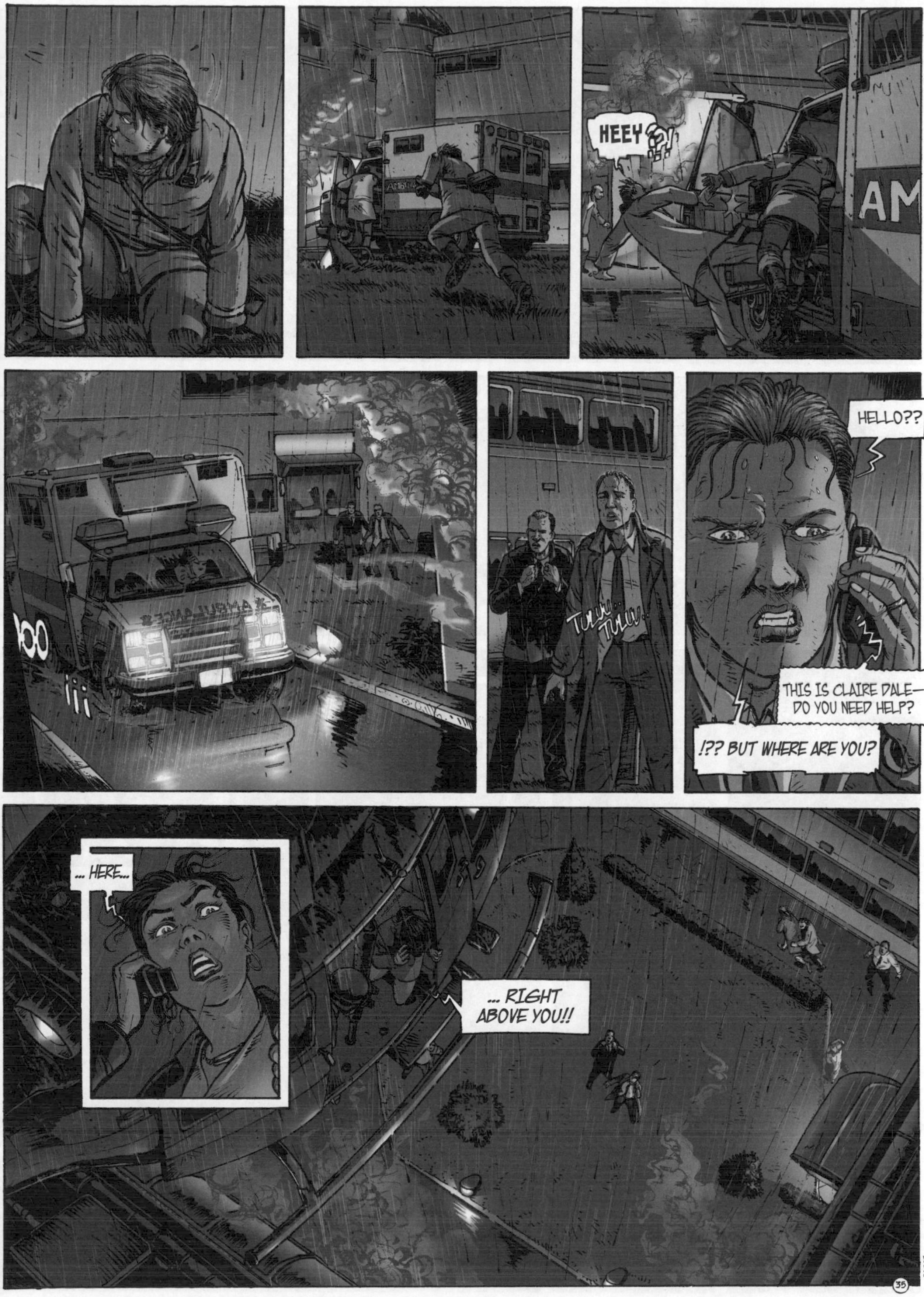
HEEY ?!
HELLO??
TULUU.. TULUU..
THIS IS CLAIRE DALE— DO YOU NEED HELP?
!?? BUT WHERE ARE YOU?
... HERE...
... RIGHT ABOVE YOU!!
35
PAGOT

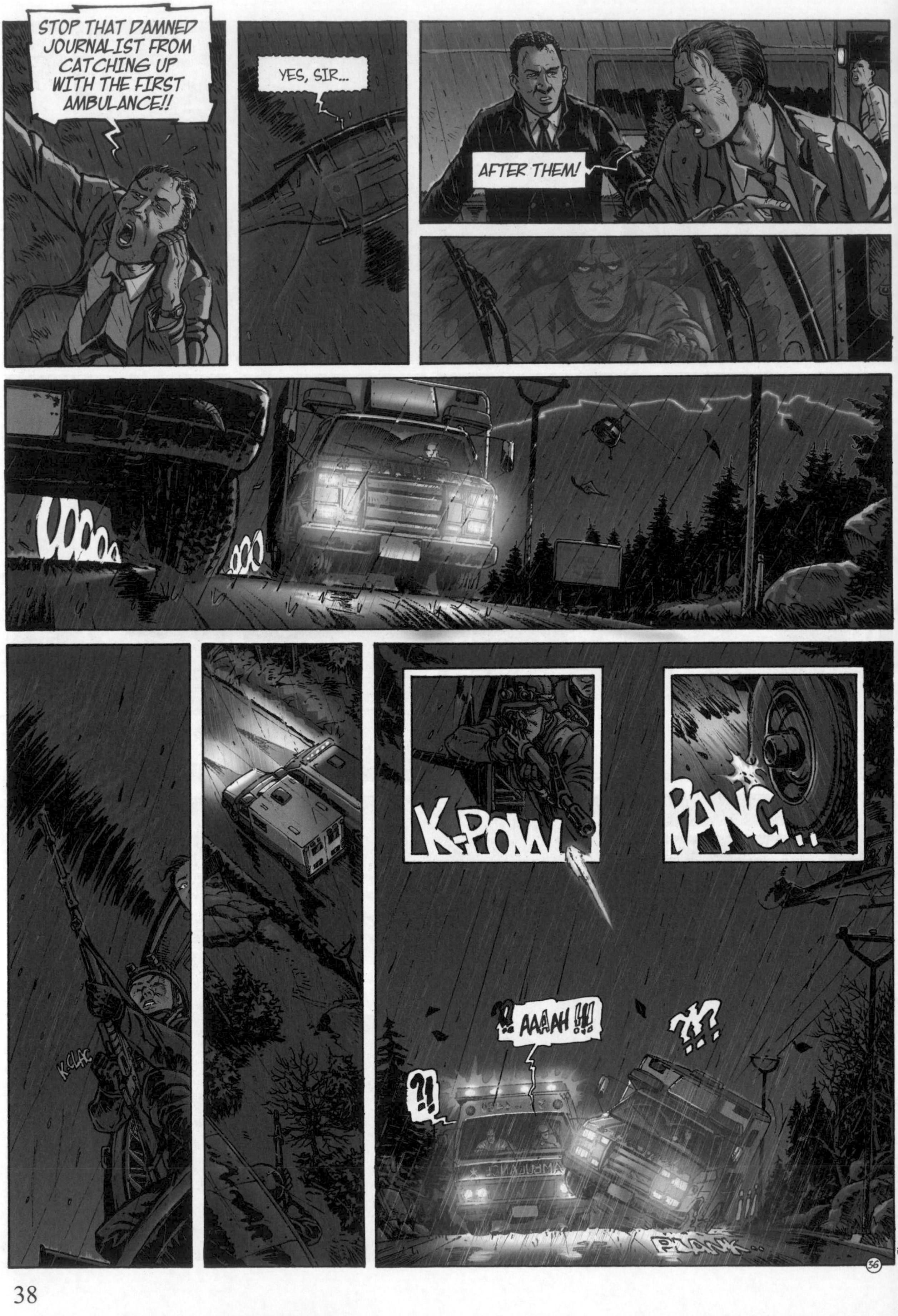
STOP THAT DAMNED JOURNALIST FROM CATCHING UP WITH THE FIRST AMBULANCE!!
YES, SIR...
AFTER THEM!
K-CLAC
K-POW
PANG..
AAAAH
PLANK..

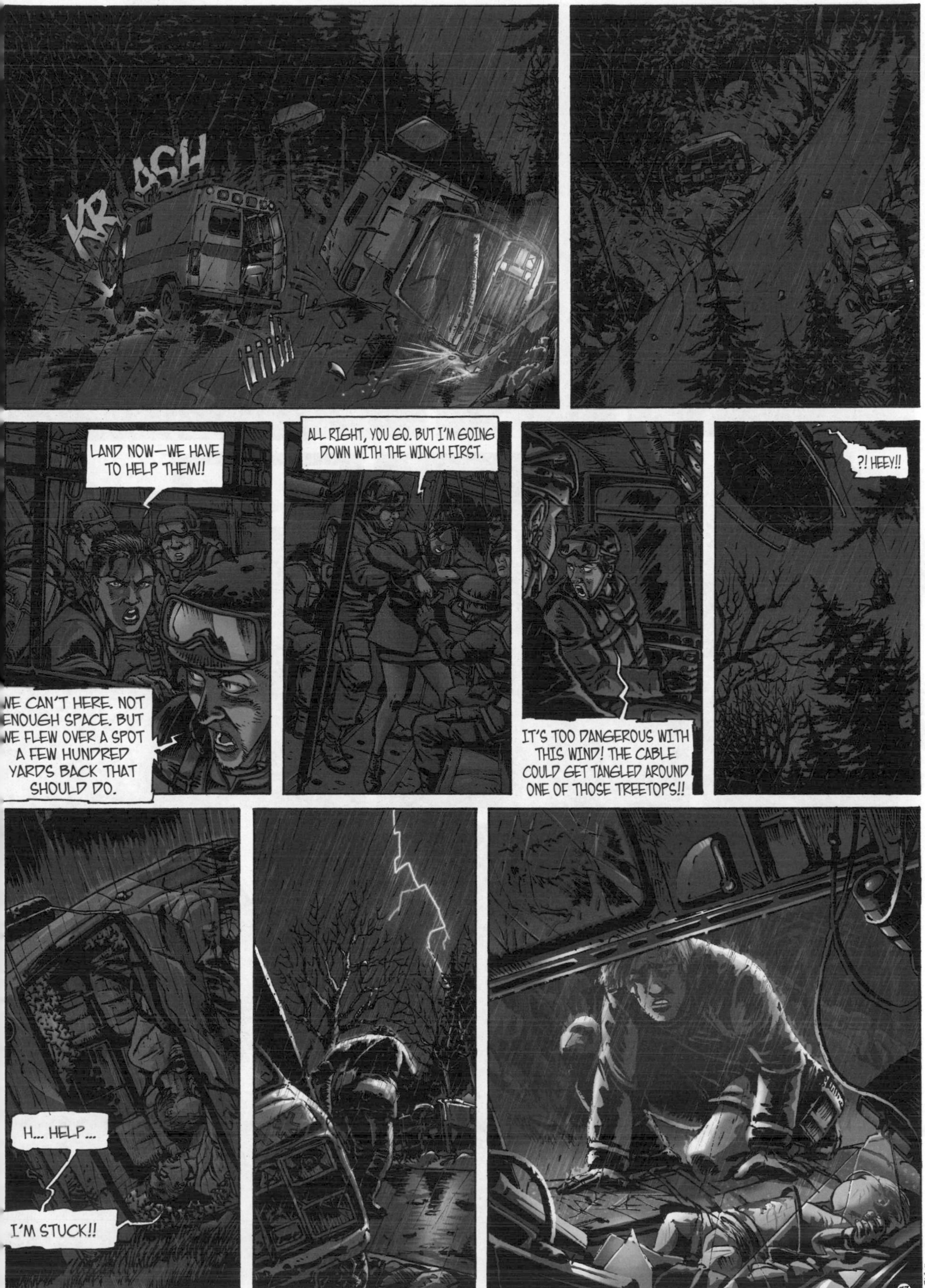
KRASH
LAND NOW—WE HAVE TO HELP THEM!!
WE CAN'T HERE. NOT ENOUGH SPACE. BUT WE FLEW OVER A SPOT A FEW HUNDRED YARDS BACK THAT SHOULD DO.
ALL RIGHT, YOU GO. BUT I'M GOING DOWN WITH THE WINCH FIRST.
IT'S TOO DANGEROUS WITH THIS WIND! THE CABLE COULD GET TANGLED AROUND ONE OF THOSE TREETOPS!!
?! HEEY!!
H... HELP...
I'M STUCK!!
37

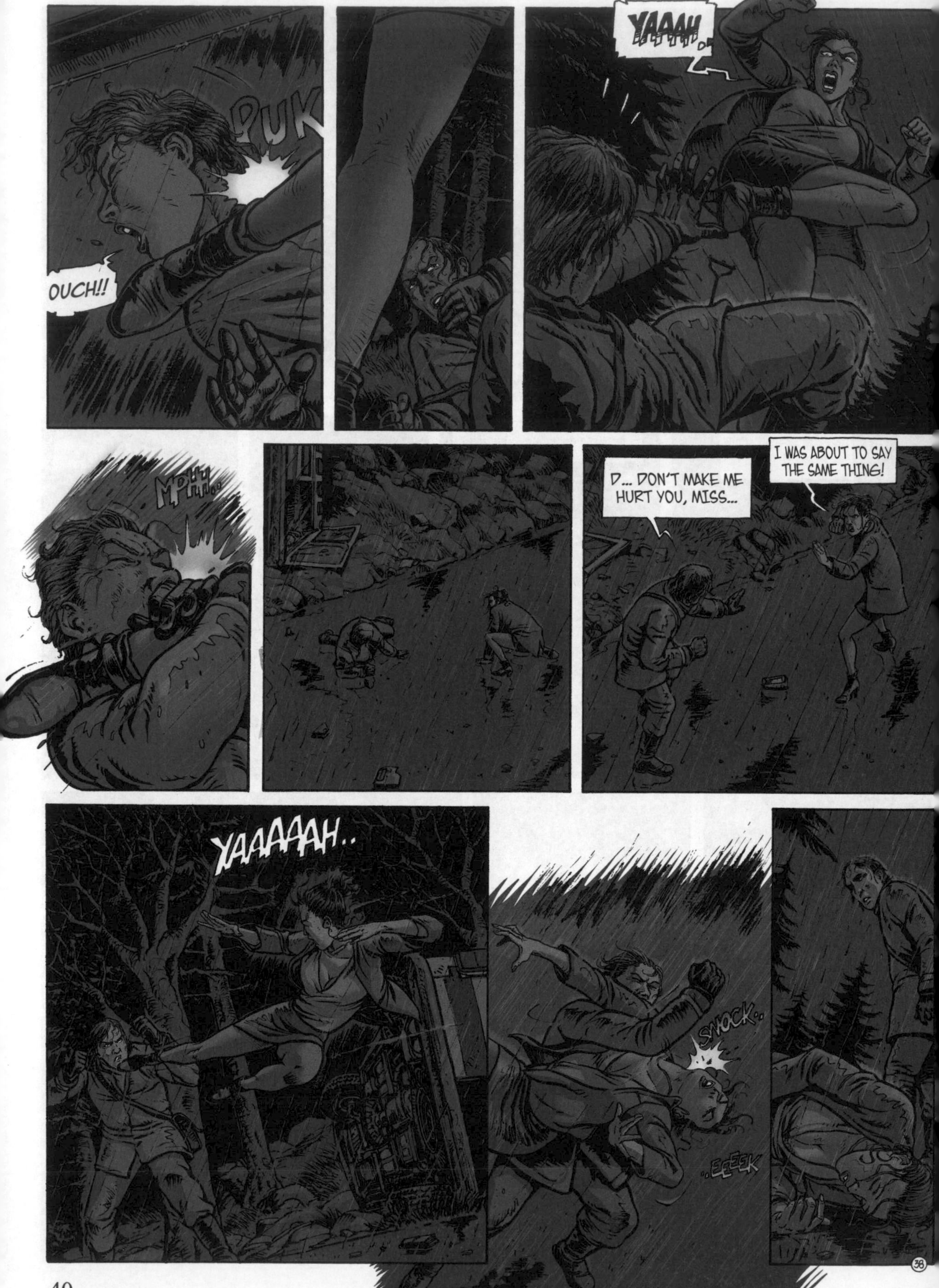
PUK
OUCH!!
YAAAH..
MPHH..
D... DON'T MAKE ME HURT YOU, MISS...
I WAS ABOUT TO SAY THE SAME THING!
YAAAAAH..
SNOCK..
..EEEEK
38

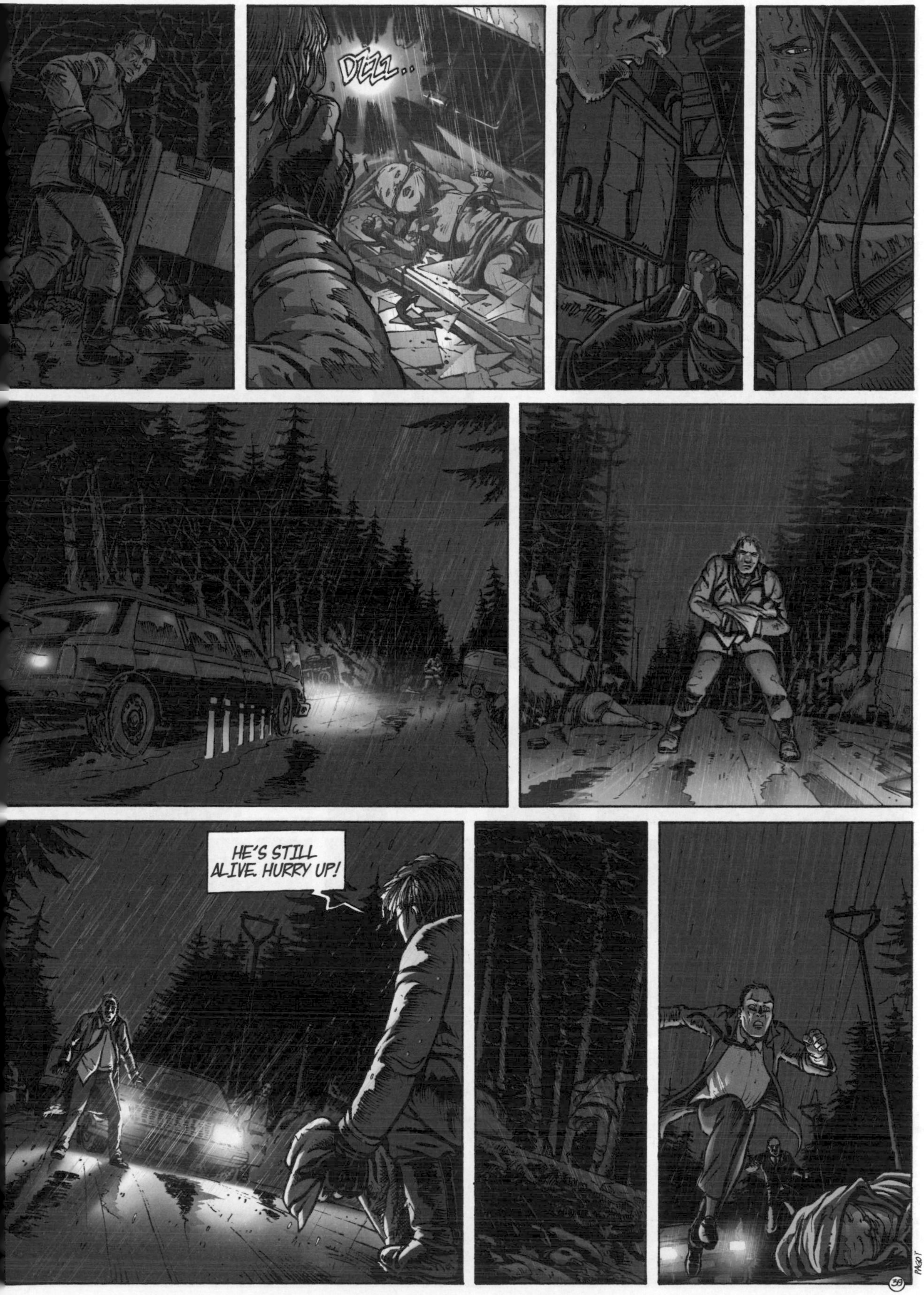
DZZZ..
HE'S STILL ALIVE. HURRY UP!

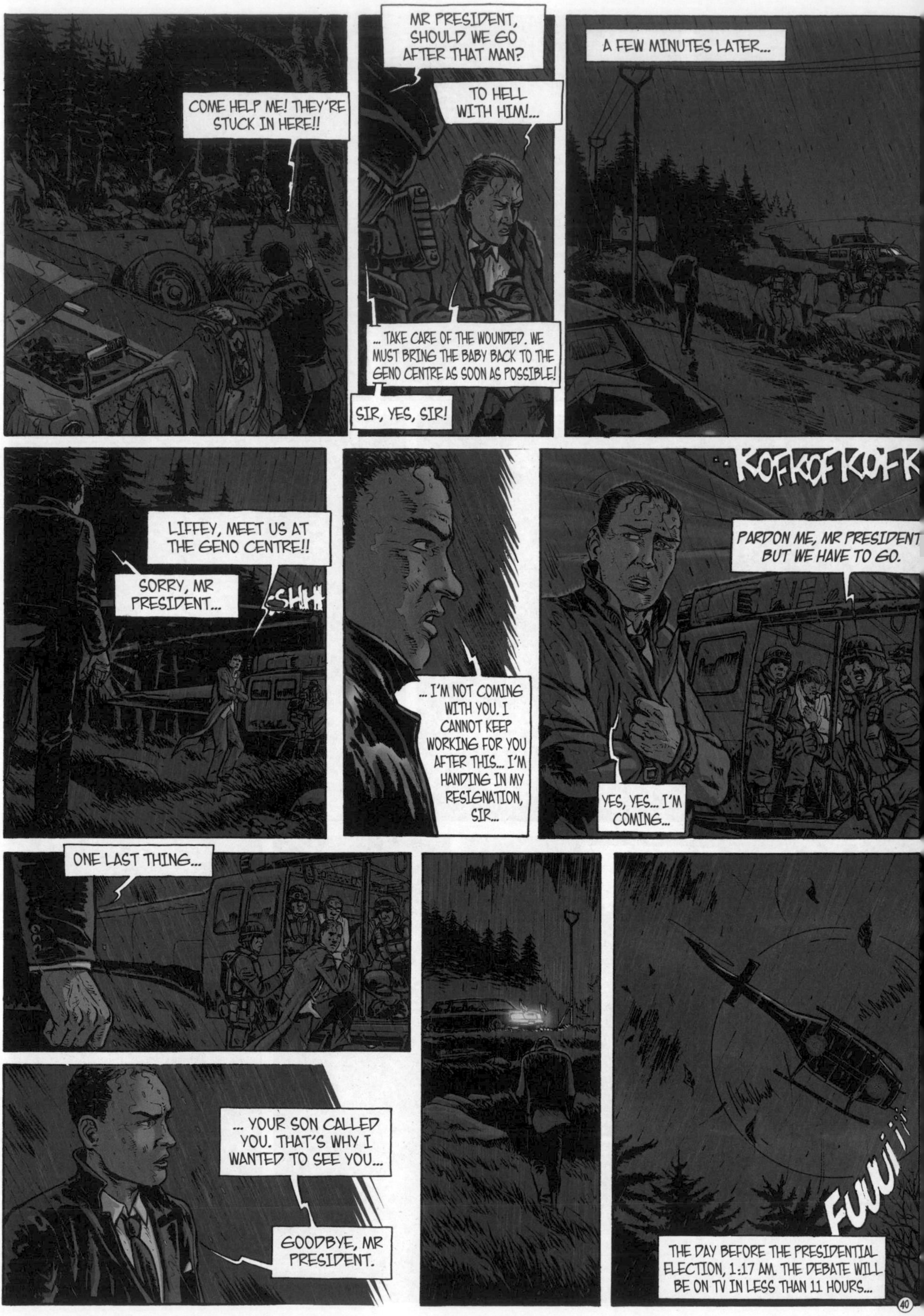
COME HELP ME! THEY'RE STUCK IN HERE!!
MR PRESIDENT, SHOULD WE GO AFTER THAT MAN?
TO HELL WITH HIM!...
... TAKE CARE OF THE WOUNDED. WE MUST BRING THE BABY BACK TO THE GENO CENTRE AS SOON AS POSSIBLE!
SIR, YES, SIR!
A FEW MINUTES LATER...
LIFFEY, MEET US AT THE GENO CENTRE!!
SORRY, MR PRESIDENT...
SHHH
... I'M NOT COMING WITH YOU. I CANNOT KEEP WORKING FOR YOU AFTER THIS... I'M HANDING IN MY RESIGNATION, SIR...
KOFKOFKOFK
PARDON ME, MR PRESIDENT BUT WE HAVE TO GO.
YES, YES... I'M COMING...
ONE LAST THING...
... YOUR SON CALLED YOU. THAT'S WHY I WANTED TO SEE YOU...
GOODBYE, MR PRESIDENT.
FUUUI
THE DAY BEFORE THE PRESIDENTIAL ELECTION, 1:17 AM. THE DEBATE WILL BE ON TV IN LESS THAN 11 HOURS...
40

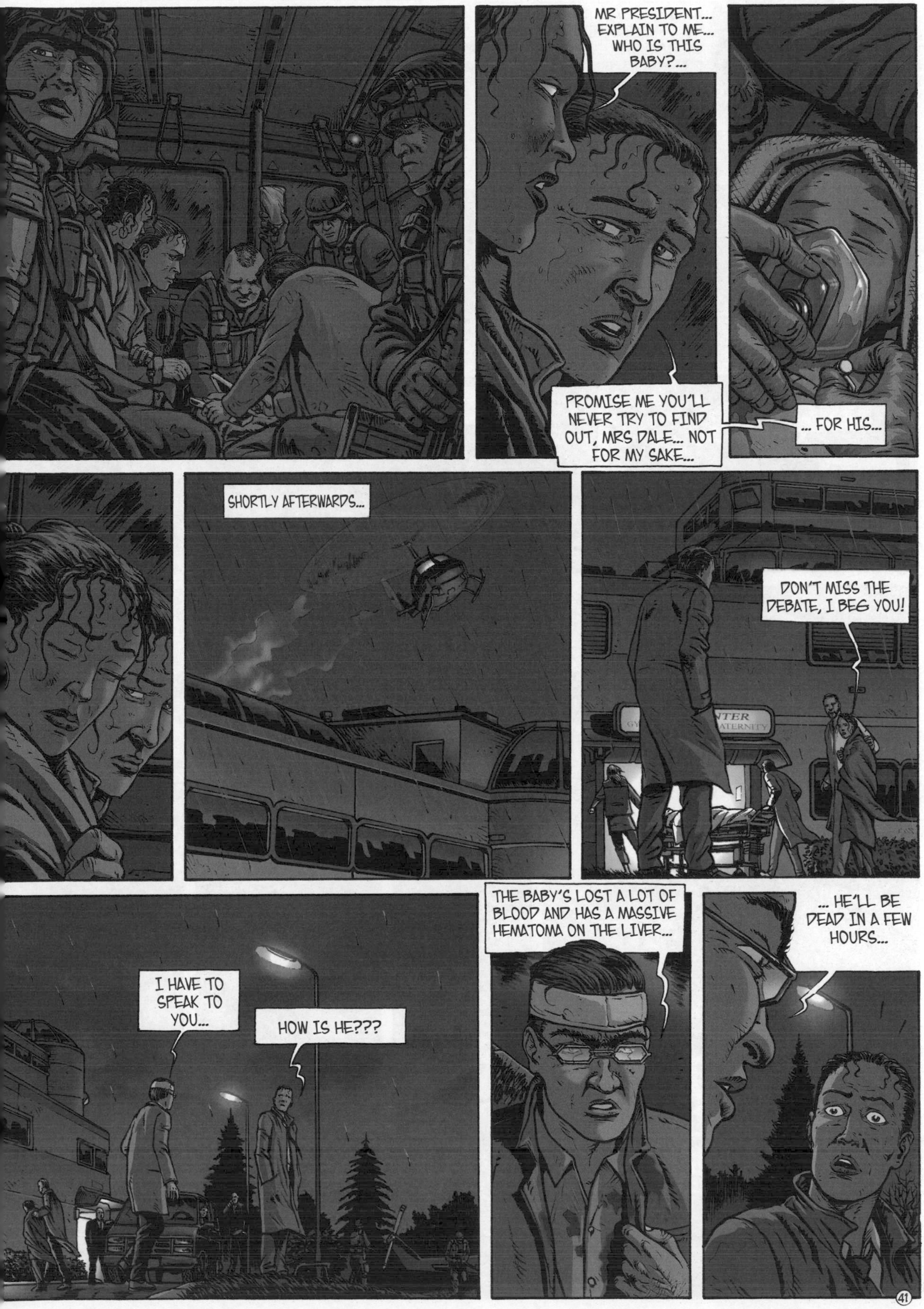
MR PRESIDENT... EXPLAIN TO ME... WHO IS THIS BABY?...
PROMISE ME YOU'LL NEVER TRY TO FIND OUT, MRS DALE... NOT FOR MY SAKE...
... FOR HIS...
SHORTLY AFTERWARDS...
DON'T MISS THE DEBATE, I BEG YOU!
I HAVE TO SPEAK TO YOU...
HOW IS HE???
THE BABY'S LOST A LOT OF BLOOD AND HAS A MASSIVE HEMATOMA ON THE LIVER...
... HE'LL BE DEAD IN A FEW HOURS...
41

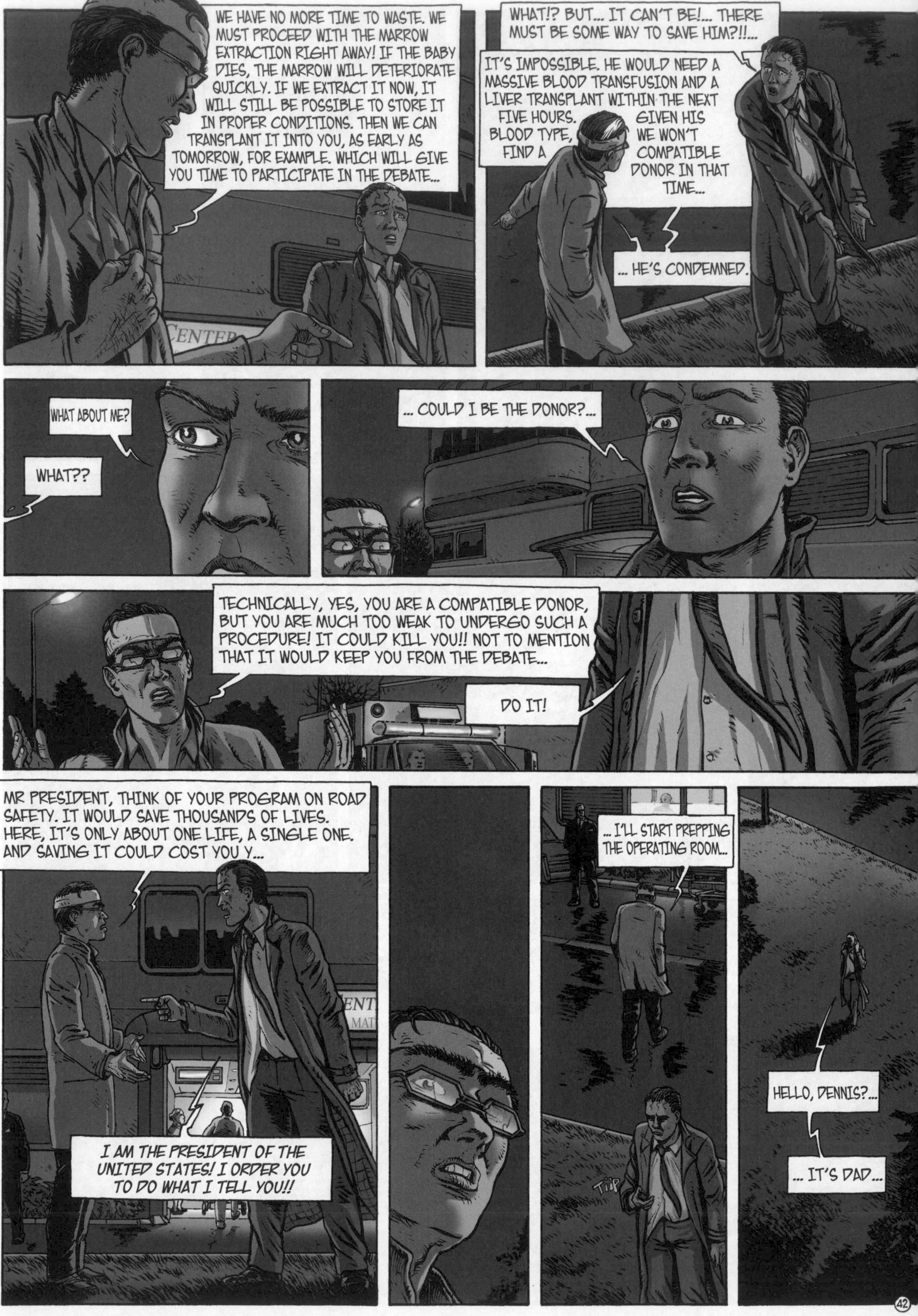
WE HAVE NO MORE TIME TO WASTE. WE MUST PROCEED WITH THE MARROW EXTRACTION RIGHT AWAY! IF THE BABY DIES, THE MARROW WILL DETERIORATE QUICKLY. IF WE EXTRACT IT NOW, IT WILL STILL BE POSSIBLE TO STORE IT IN PROPER CONDITIONS. THEN WE CAN TRANSPLANT IT INTO YOU, AS EARLY AS TOMORROW, FOR EXAMPLE. WHICH WILL GIVE YOU TIME TO PARTICIPATE IN THE DEBATE...
CENTER
WHAT!? BUT... IT CAN'T BE!... THERE MUST BE SOME WAY TO SAVE HIM?!!...
IT'S IMPOSSIBLE. HE WOULD NEED A MASSIVE BLOOD TRANSFUSION AND A LIVER TRANSPLANT WITHIN THE NEXT FIVE HOURS. GIVEN HIS BLOOD TYPE, WE WON'T FIND A COMPATIBLE DONOR IN THAT TIME...
... HE'S CONDEMNED.
WHAT ABOUT ME?
WHAT??
... COULD I BE THE DONOR?...
TECHNICALLY, YES, YOU ARE A COMPATIBLE DONOR, BUT YOU ARE MUCH TOO WEAK TO UNDERGO SUCH A PROCEDURE! IT COULD KILL YOU!! NOT TO MENTION THAT IT WOULD KEEP YOU FROM THE DEBATE...
DO IT!
MR PRESIDENT, THINK OF YOUR PROGRAM ON ROAD SAFETY. IT WOULD SAVE THOUSANDS OF LIVES. HERE, IT'S ONLY ABOUT ONE LIFE, A SINGLE ONE. AND SAVING IT COULD COST YOU Y...
I AM THE PRESIDENT OF THE UNITED STATES! I ORDER YOU TO DO WHAT I TELL YOU!!
... I'LL START PREPPING THE OPERATING ROOM...
TIIP
HELLO, DENNIS?...
... IT'S DAD...

42

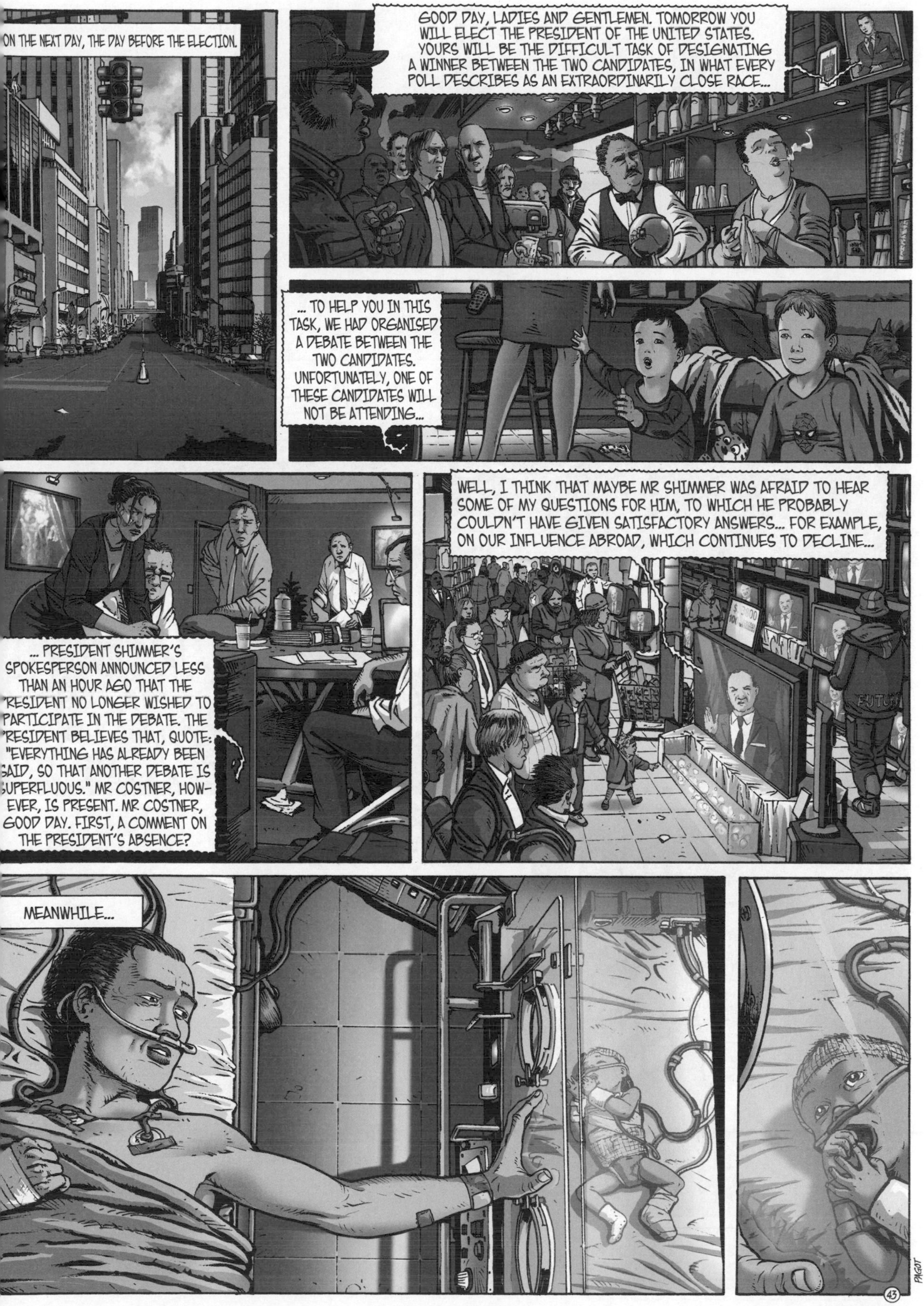

ON THE NEXT DAY, THE DAY BEFORE THE ELECTION.
GOOD DAY, LADIES AND GENTLEMEN. TOMORROW YOU WILL ELECT THE PRESIDENT OF THE UNITED STATES. YOURS WILL BE THE DIFFICULT TASK OF DESIGNATING A WINNER BETWEEN THE TWO CANDIDATES, IN WHAT EVERY POLL DESCRIBES AS AN EXTRAORDINARILY CLOSE RACE...
... TO HELP YOU IN THIS TASK, WE HAD ORGANISED A DEBATE BETWEEN THE TWO CANDIDATES. UNFORTUNATELY, ONE OF THESE CANDIDATES WILL NOT BE ATTENDING...
... PRESIDENT SHIMMER'S SPOKESPERSON ANNOUNCED LESS THAN AN HOUR AGO THAT THE RESIDENT NO LONGER WISHED TO ARTICIPATE IN THE DEBATE. THE RESIDENT BELIEVES THAT, QUOTE: "EVERYTHING HAS ALREADY BEEN AID, SO THAT ANOTHER DEBATE IS UPERFLUOUS." MR COSTNER, HOW-EVER, IS PRESENT. MR COSTNER, GOOD DAY. FIRST, A COMMENT ON THE PRESIDENT'S ABSENCE?
WELL, I THINK THAT MAYBE MR SHIMMER WAS AFRAID TO HEAR SOME OF MY QUESTIONS FOR HIM, TO WHICH HE PROBABLY COULDN'T HAVE GIVEN SATISFACTORY ANSWERS... FOR EXAMPLE, ON OUR INFLUENCE ABROAD, WHICH CONTINUES TO DECLINE...
MEANWHILE...
PAGOT
43

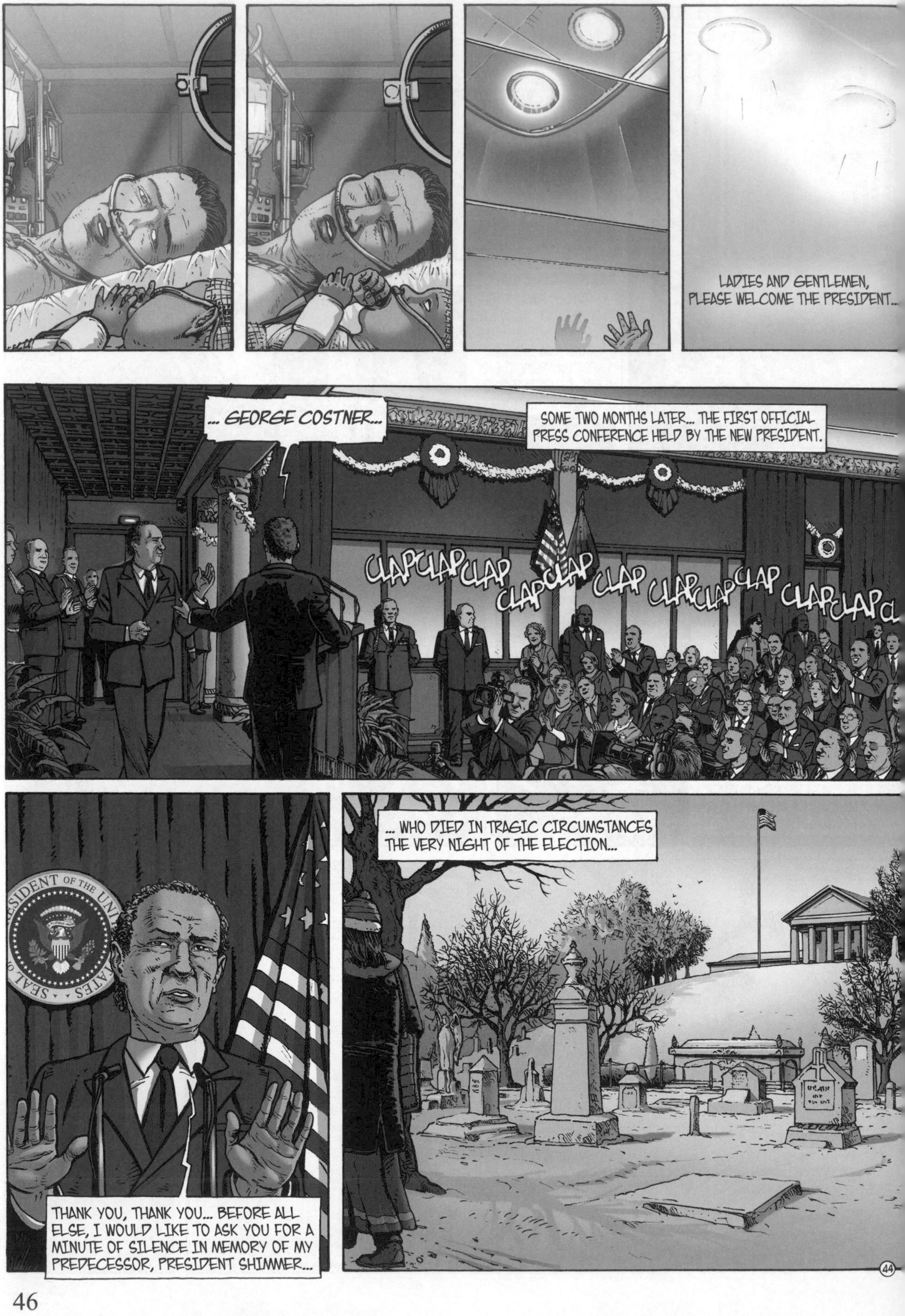
LADIES AND GENTLEMEN, PLEASE WELCOME THE PRESIDENT...
... GEORGE COSTNER...
SOME TWO MONTHS LATER... THE FIRST OFFICIAL PRESS CONFERENCE HELD BY THE NEW PRESIDENT.
CLAPCLAPCLAP
CLAPCLAP
CLAP
CLAPCLAPCLAP
CLAPCLAP
THANK YOU, THANK YOU... BEFORE ALL ELSE, I WOULD LIKE TO ASK YOU FOR A MINUTE OF SILENCE IN MEMORY OF MY PREDECESSOR, PRESIDENT SHIMMER...
... WHO DIED IN TRAGIC CIRCUMSTANCES THE VERY NIGHT OF THE ELECTION...
44

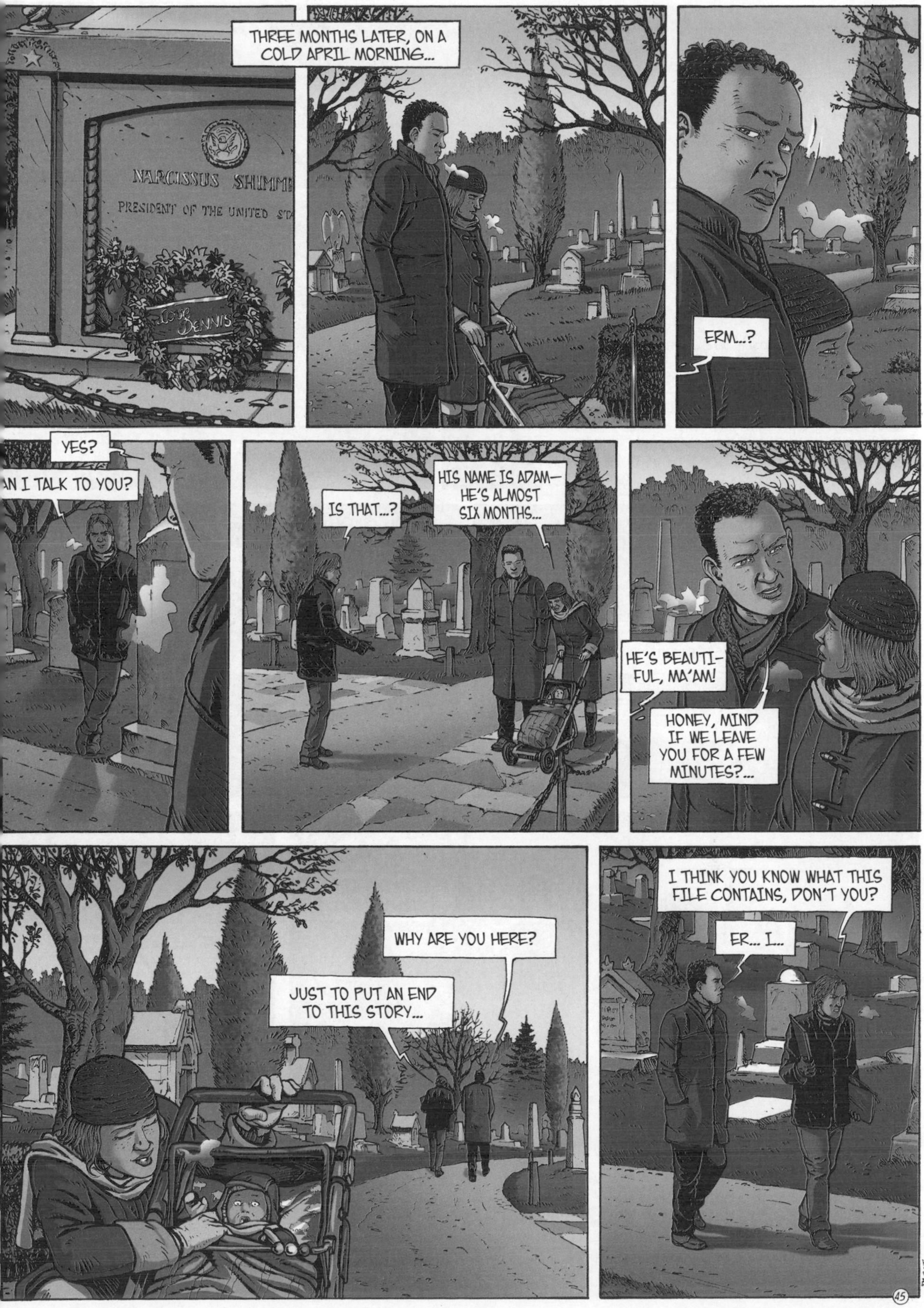
NARCISSUS SHIMM
PRESIDENT OF THE UNITED STA
THREE MONTHS LATER, ON A COLD APRIL MORNING...
ERM...?
YES?
AN I TALK TO YOU?
IS THAT...?
HIS NAME IS ADAM— HE'S ALMOST SIX MONTHS...
HE'S BEAUTI-FUL, MA'AM!
HONEY, MIND IF WE LEAVE YOU FOR A FEW MINUTES?...
WHY ARE YOU HERE?
JUST TO PUT AN END TO THIS STORY...
I THINK YOU KNOW WHAT THIS FILE CONTAINS, DON'T YOU?
ER... I...
45

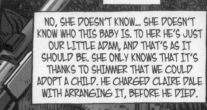

DOES SHE?

NO, SHE DOESN'T KNOW... SHE DOESN'T KNOW WHO THIS BABY IS. TO HER HE'S JUST OUR LITTLE ADAM, AND THAT'S AS IT SHOULD BE. SHE ONLY KNOWS THAT IT'S THANKS TO SHIMMER THAT WE COULD ADOPT A CHILD. HE CHARGED CLAIRE DALE WITH ARRANGING IT, BEFORE HE DIED.

BUT... WHAT ABOUT DR TURPIN?... AND YOU...?

DR TURPIN COMMITTED SUICIDE THREE WEEKS AGO. HIS COMPANY WENT BANKRUPT AND HE WAS COMPLETELY RUINED—HE WAS COUNTING FAR TOO MUCH ON THE SUBSIDIES THAT SHIMMER HAD PROMISED HIM AND THAT WERE BLOCKED BY THE OTHER PARTY. AS FOR ME, I WAS WORKING FOR COSTNER... BUT HE KNOWS NOTHING.

... I ALMOST KILLED A BABY... EVEN MUCKRAKERS CAN SOMETIMES FEEL THAT THEY WENT TOO FAR. SO I CONVINCED COSTNER THAT THE BABY HAD NOTHING TO DO WITH SHIMMER AND THAT WE'D GONE AFTER COMPLETELY THE WRONG PREY... BUT AFTER ALL, HE WAS PAYING ME TO STOP SHIMMER, AND THAT'S WHAT HAPPENED, ISN'T IT

SO THERE ARE ONLY TWO OF US LEFT WHO KNOW?

NO, MR LIFFEY...

KLIK..

SHRR..

... THERE'S ONLY YOU...

BROF

GOODBYE, MR LIFFEY...

... TAKE GOOD CARE OF ADAM...

46

SCRIPT: ALCANTE
DRAWING: D. PAGOT
COLOUR WORK: C. ARALDI

THE END...